hill Sep. 15. 1723.

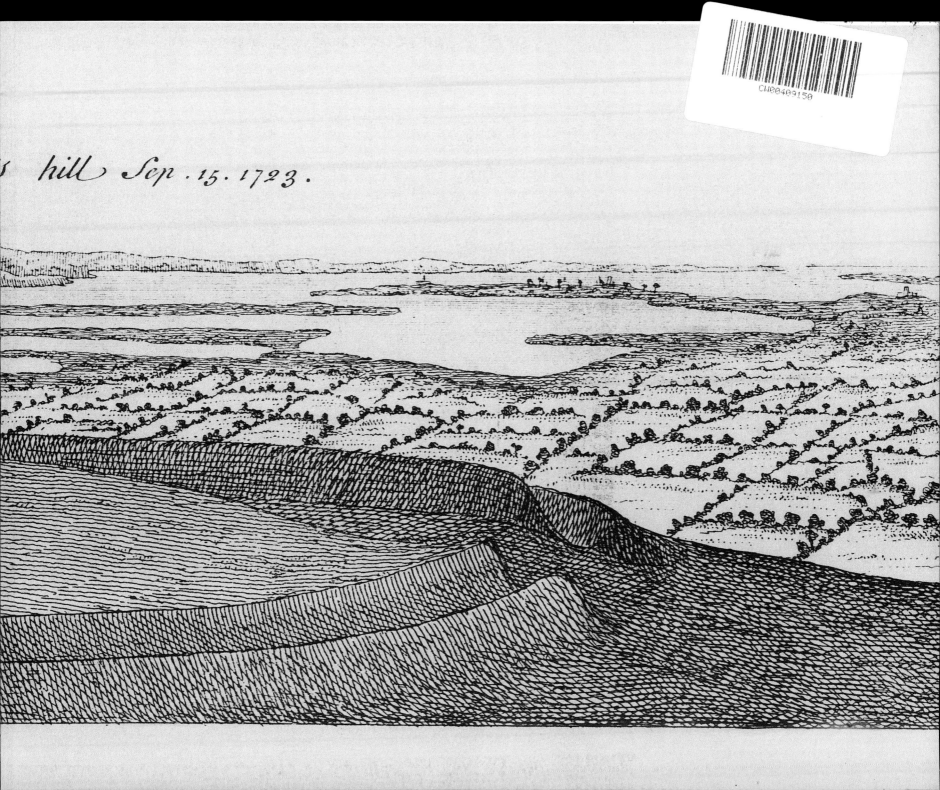

CHICHESTER

A MILLENNIUM VIEW

Richard Pailthorpe • Iain McGowan

With a Foreword by His Grace the Duke of Richmond and Gordon

JOHN WILEY & SONS, LTD
Chichester • New York • Weinheim • Brisbane • Singapore • Toronto

Other Wiley Editorial Offices
New York • Weinheim • Brisbane • Singapore • Toronto

British Library Cataloguing in Publication Data
A catalogue record for this book is available from the British
Library
ISBN 0-471-61372-X

Production: Graham Russel
Design: ArtMedia Ltd, London
Printed in Italy by Conti Tipocolor, Florence

PHOTOGRAPHIC CREDITS

All photographs by Iain McGowan FRPS except for the following:
The Boxgrove Project, University College, London p 6 (left); British
School of Ballooning p 114; Chichester District Museum Collection,
including paintings by M Codd, pp 6 (right), 7, 8, 12 (top), 13
(bottom right), 14 (right); Chichester Festivities p 53; Chichester
High School for Boys p 56 (left); Revd K W Clinch p 24 (right);
Gelatin Manufacturers of Europe p 80; K Green p 11 (bottom
right); J Mann p 142 (bottom right); National Trust Photographic
Library, (Geoff Hamilton) p 78 (left); R Pailthorpe pp 48 (left), 117
(hurdles), 117 (sheep), 144 (bottom left, centre and right); Pallant
House p 40 (bottom right); Portsmouth Publishing and Printing
Ltd, pp 13 (top left), 14 (left), 17 (left and centre), 56 (right), 57
(all), 60 (right), 65 (bottom right), 91 (top), 182 (right), 183 (both),
189 (both); C Simon Sykes p 143 (both); St Richard's Hospital p 64;
Sussex Archaeological Society (Fishbourne Roman Palace), p 16
(bottom right); Mrs J Sutherland p 185; J Timbers p 51 (right);
Trustees of the Goodwood Collection p 10 (both); D Turner pp 16
(bottom left), 188 (bottom left); West Sussex County Council
Library Service p 9; West Sussex Record Office pp 12 (bottom left),
12 (right), 13 (top three left), 16 (top right), 12 (centre) – W Kevis
Collection; Mrs J Whiting pp 15 (bottom left), 48 (right), 58
(right), 117 (pig and bottom left), 138 (bottom left), 147, 174
(bottom left), 188 (bottom right); Mrs D Zeuner p 117 (horses).

CONTENTS

FOREWORD

BY HIS GRACE THE TENTH DUKE OF RICHMOND

I SUPPOSE it makes sense for me to write this Foreword, for my family have now lived just outside Chichester at Goodwood for slightly over 300 years. All during that time, we have been closely involved in the life of the city, and in constructing and maintaining many of its historic buildings.

The Third Duke (I am the Tenth) built the Council Chamber in North Street and the old theatre in South Street. Several Dukes contributed to the repair of the market cross at regular intervals, and as for the cathedral!

I always say that there is an entry in the family history every thirty years or so, saying 'The Dean called on His Grace'! When the spire of the cathedral fell down in 1861, the Duke of Norfolk, the Duke of Richmond, and the Earl of Leconfield met some two weeks later and settled the cost of re-erecting it! What with taxation of various kinds, it is not the same today! However, I was myself, for six years, Chairman of the Cathedral Trust, which for many years now has raised about £350,000 per annum to sustain the restoration of the cathedral fabric.

Even the Chichester Festival Theatre built in 1962, and very much a 1960s design, has recently been scheduled as a Grade I listed building. However, Chichester is not just historic buildings, important as they are. Chichester is a cultural centre with the Theatre, the Pallant House Gallery, and the Festivities – the annual arts festival.

Also vital is the atmosphere of the city. It is a relatively small place (only 25,000 residents), laid out into four main streets since Roman times, economically very prosperous, with excellent schools, and many tourist attractions and leisure facilities. There are a fair number of retired people who have looked at the potential of other attractive towns and other cathedral cities but, in the end, they chose Chichester for their retirement.

This is not just another millennium book! It is different because it is about a small and beautiful city whose residents love to live there. I am sure you will see why, when you read it and look at these pictures. Let all Cicestrians do their utmost in the next one hundred to one thousand years to ensure that Chichester remains the place we all want to continue to live in or near.

INTRODUCTION

DURING the 21st century Chichester will enter its third millennium, having grown from a Roman military base to a cathedral city and the county town of West Sussex. It is one of the country's smallest cities with a population of only 25,000 and within its defensive walls nearly 2,000 years of change and development are revealed. Wars and political events of national significance have rarely had any impact, despite the efforts of Parliamentarian troops and the Luftwaffe to leave their mark.

A true prospect of the city and its locality can be gained by standing on St Roche's Hill, a few miles to the north, which overlooks Goodwood Racecourse and is better known as the Trundle. From the ramparts of this former Iron Age fort one of southern England's most panoramic views unfolds in every direction. The long line of the South Downs stretches formidably to the north, with the densely wooded slopes of Charlton Forest in the foreground, but to the south one's eye is irresistibly drawn towards the cathedral spire. In the autumn, it can rise in ghostly fashion above an early morning mist and on a clear day it stands majestically over the flat fertile coastal plain, with the glistening inlets of Chichester Harbour, the Sussex coast, Spithead, and the Isle of Wight on the horizon beyond. The spire, the third tallest in England, acts as a landmark for any traveller, and it has the unique distinction of being the only cathedral spire to be visible from the sea. The photographs for this book have been selected to reflect not only the story of Chichester, but also to give a portrait of present day life in the city and its surrounding district, including the market towns of Petworth and Midhurst at this celebrated moment in modern history. The pictures complement those taken in our previous book *Chichester: A Contemporary View* and capture the beauty of the contrasting local landscapes from the Weald and the Downs to the coast and harbour as well as the architecture, events and people that residents and visitors will associate with the area. Whilst old photographs are able to give us a pictorial image of how things have changed during the last one hundred or so years, Mike Codd's detailed reconstruction paintings on pages 6, 7 and 8 are able to take us much further back in time to show how Chichester may have appeared.

Although the origins of the Chichester we associate with today can be traced back to the Roman occupation, archaeological evidence of man's earlier existence in the area abounds. In 1993 a discovery of international importance was made when archaeologists discovered a shin bone which was dated as 500,000 years old. The tibia belonged to a species called *Homo heidelbergensis* or 'Boxgrove Man', as its owner became known.

The attractions of the Trundle as a defensive site are still clearly visible today. It was first occupied sometime between 5000 and 4000 BC during the Neolithic period and was an important Iron Age fort from the 4th century BC until its abandonment in about 100 BC. On the slopes below, other settlements dating from the Neolithic period, the Bronze Age and Iron Age have recently been revealed. During the building of the A27 Westhampnett bypass in the early 1990s a range of discoveries were made spanning 10,000 years of human occupation. It is open to speculation whether a main Iron Age settlement still remains to be found and it seems likely that the Romans would have encountered a number of settlements based on farming and cross-channel trade.

We know little about what life or expectations may have been like for

Mark Roberts, project director (right), with Geoffrey Wainwright, chief archaeologist at English Heritage, holding the tibia bone beside the excavations at Boxgrove.

Boxgrove Man was probably about 35 years old at the time of his death, more than six feet tall and weighed more than 14 stone. The climate at this time would have been temperate and the site is on the edge of what was once the Goodwood–Slindon raised beach, rising some 100 feet above the present sea level. The beach probably extended from Portsdown in the west to the River Arun in the east. Evidence reveals that these people's diet included rhinoceros, red deer and bear. The remains of a horse, whose bones had been broken up to extract marrow for nourishment, were also found. Tools would have been made from flint worked from the cliff face and used for butchering the animals.

It has been speculated that the Romans may have landed at Chichester Harbour and used Fishbourne as a bridgehead during the invasion in AD 43. The local tribe, the Atrebates were friendly towards the Romans and their king, Tiberius Claudius Togidubnus, was possibly the builder of the magnificent palace at Fishbourne. By the time of his death towards the end of the 1st century, Roman Chichester – Noviomagus Reg(i)norum – had become established as a *civitas* or capital of the local kingdom. The region must have enjoyed a great deal of prosperity during the next three centuries and this is reflected in the remains of a number of villas discovered in the surrounding countryside, not only at Bignor, but also to the north in the Chilgrove valley

The picture portrays the town at about AD 100. An amphitheatre and cemetery occupied sites outside on the eastern approach, adjoining Stane Street, the road to Londinium (London). Consecrated graves of richer people would have been placed near to the road and would have had grand tombstones. The road northwards led to Calleva Atrebatum (Silchester) and a further road led southwards to Selsey Bill. The town had a number of important buildings including a forum, basilica, public baths, *macellum* and a temple dedicated to Neptune and Minerva. Large areas would have at this time been devoid of buildings and people would largely have lived in timber-framed houses. A straight road can be seen leading directly to Fishbourne.

The Roman city walls were not built for at least another 200 years. Whilst the main streets are similar to their present-day alignment, the overall street plan of today's Chichester is based on its Saxon layout.

those living in Saxon Chichester at the turn of the last millennium. The Romans had left Britain at the beginning of the 5th century, and within 50 years Sussex had been colonised by the invading Saxons, whose leader was Aella. It is debatable whether the name Chichester is derived from one of Aella's sons called Cissa, who it is said renamed the former Roman town 'Cissa's ceaster' meaning 'Cissa's camp'. After St Wilfrid had converted the south Saxons to Christianity at the end of the 7th century, Selsey, and not Chichester, became the most important cultural centre in the region with the building of its cathedral church. A Christian community, pre-dating St Wilfrid, had been established at Bosham, and during the first half of the new millennium, Bosham was to become well known for its associations with King Harold, depicted on the Bayeux Tapestry praying in the church before sailing to Normandy in 1064.

The Anglo-Saxon Chronicle records that the townsmen of Chichester, or more probably a force of local men, defeated a Danish army in 894. The town was one of five Saxon fortifications in Sussex known as *burhs* and its Roman walls must have been still considered an important defence against the threat of attack from marauding Danes. The present city street plan originates from the Saxon period and timber-framed buildings must have replaced the former Roman public and civic ones. Chichester did have a mint and it is recorded that there was a nunnery dedicated to St Peter, which probably stood on the site of the cathedral. Many of today's place names are Saxon in origin and the remains of masonry in a number of village churches points towards a settlement pattern which can still be traced back to the Saxons.

After the Conquest, the rape of Chichester was granted to Earl Roger de Montgomery. Nevertheless, it was the transfer of the bishop's seat from Selsey in 1075 that changed the course of the city's history. The Domesday Survey in 1086 mentions that 60 more houses had been built since 1066. During the medieval period Chichester became not only a pilgrimage and spiritual centre, but also an important port and market town. Its population probably did not fluctuate much throughout the medieval period and has been estimated to have been between 1,200 and 1,500.

William the Conqueror divided Sussex into administrative districts known as 'rapes'. The rapes of Chichester and Arundel were granted to Roger de Montgomery, who erected motte and bailey castles at Arundel and Chichester. The castle erected in the north-east corner of Chichester's walls was possibly never more than a timber construction. The illustration depicts how it may have looked shortly after the Conquest in 1066. We know a little about its history and that at the end of the 12th century it was garrisoned by five knights and victualled with barley, beans and bacon, indicating the threat of siege. This was the result of John's attempt to seize the throne whilst his brother Richard I was in captivity. In 1216 the castle was captured by Prince Louis, the French dauphin, during the barons' war with King John. The following year, after John's death, it was re-taken and orders were given to raze it to the ground.

The remains of the motte, or earthen mound, can still be seen in Priory Park, but it has been much reduced in height over the years and the surrounding ditch was filled in after the castle went out of use.

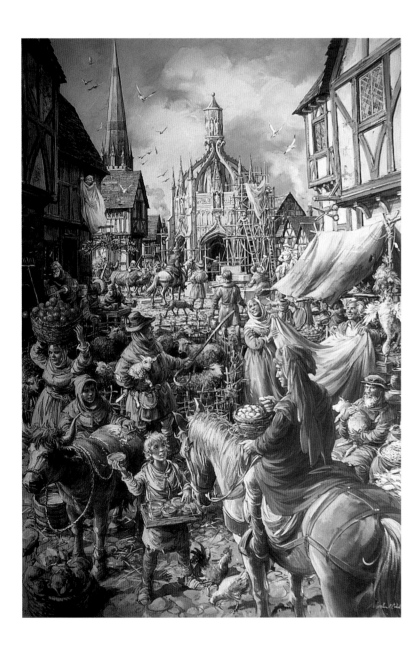

Whilst archaeology and buildings can give us clues to Chichester's past, it is only during the last 500 years that we can rely on contemporary accounts which reflect its contrasting fortunes. By the end of the 16th century, despite a royal visit from Queen Elizabeth I in 1591, the city is recorded as being in a decayed state. Descriptions over a century later by James Spershott, a local resident, indicate that there had been little change when he remarks about the city's 'mean appearance'. However, during Spershott's lifetime (which spanned much of the 18th century) the city enjoyed a major period of prosperity and many of the splendid Georgian buildings we treasure today were re-modelled or built at this time. This new-found wealth was based on local agriculture and in particular a flourishing trade in grain and sheep farming. By 1831 the population had risen to more than 8,000; and it is interesting to reflect that the meat and fish paste business of C. Shippam Ltd was founded during the Georgian era in 1750 and still thrives today. The period also saw the development of the great country estates, notably at Goodwood and Petworth, under the inspired and visionary directions of the third Duke of Richmond and the third Earl of Egremont.

A conjectural view of East Street at the beginning of the 16th century during the construction of the market cross. The street is bustling with traders and sheep, and is flanked by jettied timber-framed buildings, inns and shops.

Work had continued throughout the medieval period on the building of the cathedral and its associated ecclesiastical buildings in the south-west quadrant. The friaries of the Greyfriars and the Blackfriars were located in the present-day Priory Park and in the south-east quadrant respectively. St Mary's Hospital was built at the end of the 13th century in the north-east quadrant.

Chichester prospered during the medieval period as a market town. A Merchants Guild Charter had been granted in 1135 and despite its distance from the sea, it was classed as a port and wool staple, entitling it to collect customs duties.

During the 14th and 15th centuries the traders and innkeepers prospered from pilgrims visiting the shrine of St Richard of Wych in the cathedral. The guild, however, was able to exercise restrictive practices over the poorer tradesmen. This led to the market cross being built by Bishop Story in 1501 as a gift to them; creating a market place where they could sell their goods free from local taxes and the threat of interference from adjoining houses and stalls being built. His deed of gift reads: 'To the Sucoure and Comfort of the Poore Peple there ...'

By the mid 1830s, Chichester had enjoyed a century of prosperity and during this time its former timber-framed buildings had been rebuilt or re-fronted. The Revd Alexander Hay in his history of Chichester published in 1804 records, 'The dwelling-houses in the four principal streets, in that part called the Pallant, and the greatest part of those in the Little-London, are above mediocrity. In the North-street in particular, though none of them have any pretence to grandeur, they are large, neat, clean and pleasant'.

Hay comments on the buildings' lack of uniformity and it is this individuality which is such a unique feature of Georgian Chichester. Some splendid examples of domestic and public architecture can be seen in the main streets as well as in St Martin's Square, Lion Street, St John's Street and most notably the Pallants.

To the south of the city the canal was built in 1822, connecting the city with the harbour at Dell Quay and the region's network of inland waterways and canals. The city suburbs also started to spread to Somerstown in the north and further along St Pancras to the east. At the beginning of the 19th century, Chichester market was the second largest in the country after Smithfield as a result of its close proximity to Portsmouth and the need to supply the naval dockyard. The above print shows hurdle pens of sheep in East Street on a market day.

The countryside to the north of Chichester today remains, despite the constant threat from an ever-increasing and more mobile population, remarkably unspoilt. This is a landscape rich in variety, which is reflected in its buildings and scenery, as the Lavant valley and wooded slopes of the chalk Downland gives way to the Rother valley and pockets of heathland, before entering the Weald. Here can be found small hedgerowed pastures, and remnants of the ancient woodland that once fuelled the Wealden glass and iron industries during the 16th and 17th centuries. The Downs and surrounding countryside influenced many distinguished poets and writers, including Tennyson, Hilaire Belloc, W.H. Hudson and E.V. Lucas. Away from the main roads a network of sunken lanes and byways reminiscent of a bygone age still connect remote villages and hamlets, medieval churches, isolated pubs and farmsteads. One of the principal reasons for the area's preservation can be attributed to the careful stewardship of the major estates such as Goodwood, West Dean, Cowdray and Petworth, which between them still own some 20,000 hectares of the land. The Dukes of Richmond have, through their participation and patronage of local affairs, had a major influence on Chichester, as have the Egremont and Cowdray families on Petworth and Midhurst. Goodwood is renowned for its association with horse racing, which was first started in 1801. During the last few years the Earl of March has introduced the extremely popular Festival of Speed event and revived motor racing on the famous Goodwood circuit.

Chichester's population had almost doubled during the 19th century and in 1901 was nearly 9,000, although much of this increase took place during the first half of the century. Despite its continuing importance as a market centre for the surrounding countryside, descriptions of the city at the end of the century are disparaging: varying from 'smelly' and 'sleepy' to 'fast losing its charming old-world appearance and character'. Perhaps the most noteworthy incident of national interest during the Victorian era was the collapse of the cathedral spire in 1861.

A view of Goodwood Racecourse between the two World Wars from Trundle Hill. Crowds in excess of 25,000 regularly watched the racing from here at this time and on average 80,000 people attended the then four-day meeting at the end of July. Attendances after the Second World War increased dramatically, reaching a record in 1953 when 62,000 watched from the Trundle alone and 150,000 attended the meeting. Today about 100,000 people attend the now five-day July meeting.

Juan Manuel Fangio, regarded by many as the greatest motor racing champion, lines up the BRM V16 on pole position for the 1953 Woodcote Cup at Goodwood

These views of North Street show how during the last two centuries sheep and cattle have given way firstly to motor transport and in modern times to pedestrians. The livestock or 'beast' market took place every other Wednesday and was held in the main streets until 1870. In North Street and East Street the hurdle pens containing the animals stretched along the streets as far as the market cross. Traders were empowered to sell 'Flesh, Meat, and other raw victuals, Fish Poultry, Rabbits, Suckling Pigs, Eggs, Butter, Herbs, Roots or other Vegetables, Fruit, China, Glass and Earthenware and such things as are usually sold in Public Markets'. The dirt and congestion created by the market led to the present market site being opened in 1871. In 1904 E.V. Lucas wrote 'Chichester is a perfect example of an English rural capital, thronged on market days with tilt carts, each bringing a farmer or farmer's wife and rich in those well-stored ironmonger's shops that one never sees elsewhere'. Cars competed with shoppers until pedestrianisation of these streets during the late 1970s, thus creating a safe and attractive environment for everyone to enjoy today.

Chichester – a century ago. A view of East Street looking eastwards, and one of North Street showing the Royal Sussex Regiment in 1901. They are marching to the railway station, en route to South Africa to fight in the Boer War, led on horseback by Colonel, the Earl of March, and Colonel Godman.

Arguably, the greatest changes to have taken place have occurred during the second half of the 20th century, yet when put into proportion these changes are perhaps no more dramatic than those experienced by the local population when the Romans arrived or the Normans began to build the cathedral. The post-war years have seen the gradual demise of many family businesses and shops and the closure of industries such as the wool-staplers (Ebenezer Prior), the tanners (Gibbings Harrison) and the brewers (Henty and Constable). The building of new housing estates had begun just prior to the Second World War and continued after it with for example Swanfield Drive, the development of Parklands and the gradual growth of Summersdale. The 1950s saw the opening of the Terminus Road industrial estate and the building of a new bus station and refurbished railway station.

Historic views of (left) Lombard Street, Petworth showing St Mary's church spire (taken down in 1947); and North Street, Midhurst (right).

The demolition of Somerstown and Westgate, together with the construction of the Avenue de Chartres through the Westgate fields during the mid 1960s.

In 1974 Christopher Fry wrote a sonnet for the Chichester Society which captured the feelings of many Cicestrians concerned over what had happened to their city during the previous decade. It is reproduced here with Christopher Fry's kind permission:

What can be said of the spoiler of cities?
  The perpetrator of a thousand pities,
Who, like the drunken surgeon with a knife,
  Thinking to cure, cuts out the life –
Who banishes, with gesture brief and graphic,
  Whatever charm disturbs the flow of traffic –
Whose lips compress, whose cardiac centre hardens
  To see a city's heart alight with hidden gardens?
What can be said of him who sees no stature
  In the uniqueness of a city's nature?
'Alas' is easily said; but no sigh pays the cost
  Of dignity destroyed and beauty lost.
And nothing then can reinstate
A city that we cared about too late.

Christopher Fry

The boarded-up shop front of H.J. Petto. Although the business only closed a few years ago, the surrounding area which was partially developed in the 1960s has become like an island surrounded by the Northgate gyratory system.

In addition, the growth of county hall, the closure of the cattle market and the development of out-of-town shopping, together with the construction of inner ring roads and gyratory systems around the former city gateways all contributed to these changes. The motor car had started to make an impression on the city before the First World War, but the bypass (now the A27) was not built until 1939. Vehicles still drove through the main streets, somehow miraculously not damaging the market cross, until pedestrianisation was introduced in the late 1970s.

Chichester, like the majority of historic towns and cities, has suffered from some ill-conceived and controversial planning decisions particularly in the 1960s. The demolition of much of the Georgian suburb of Somerstown and other traditional buildings within the city walls and the construction of the Avenue de Chartres through the Westgate fields led in the 1970s to a growing concern amongst Cicestrians over the future of their environment and architectural heritage. There will always be controversial developments, and more major schemes in and around the city are proposed for the new millennium. However, public opinion and a more enlightened approach to conservation planning have helped to redress the balance.

Derek Bowerman, Stride's auctioneer, on almost the final day of the cattle market before it closed on 24th October 1990.

As well as performing its spiritual, administrative and commercial roles, it is as a centre for arts and culture that Chichester has built its reputation in modern times, with the internationally famous Festival Theatre and the annual arts festival, known as the Chichester Festivities. Apart from its Georgian architecture, the discovery of the Fishbourne Roman Palace, the creation of the Weald and Downland Open Air Museum at Singleton, and the restoration of Pallant House as an historic house and art gallery have all contributed to Chichester becoming an important heritage and tourist destination. During the new millennium a number of projects involving the arts and heritage, charities, sports and community-based schemes (such as millennium events, village halls and parish map groups) will have benefited from National Lottery funding.

During the intervening years and continuing to the present day, the face of Chichester's shops have gradually changed from the small specialised family businesses to mainly nationally branded retailers. It is an impossible task to mention all of those shops and businesses which have closed during the last 50 years, but the following are just some whose names will be familiar to many Cicestrians, and are drawn from personal memory.

The International Stores, Harris and Hall, Sharp Garland, Pinks, Liptons and Maypole (grocers and general stores); Charlie Howard, Kimbells, Elphicks (butchers); Barbers, Byerleys, MacFisheries (fishmongers); Orchard Stores, Priors (fruiterers); W. Bartholomew, Lewis, Mickeys (tobacconists); Perrings (furniture supplier); C.C. Allen, Faiths, Lewis (jewellers); Sidney Bastow, G. Bevis, Binns, Savory Moore, Timothy Whites (chemists); T. Jay, G. Pine (ironmongers); Charges (ladies' fashion); Bishops, Griffith Bros, Guy Reynolds, Turnbulls (men's outfitters); Geerings, Domans, Penneys, Shirleys (haberdashery and materials); Clarks, Smurthwaites (paint suppliers); Russell Hillsdon, Linkins (sports and games); Martlet Toys; Barretts, The Wessex, Meynells (bookshops); Hoopers (florist); Storrys (musical instruments and records); Chittys, Daniels, Lummus (electrical goods); Fielders, Rapsons, Finlays (newsagents); Andrews (cycles); Petto (shoe repairs); Bartholomews, Combes, Sadlers (garden stores and animal feeds); Chaffers, Laceys, and Moore and Tillyer (printing businesses).

All four main streets had garage premises – Adcocks (East Street), Masons, Wadhams, Fields (South Street), Blue Star, Popes (North Street), Reed's (West Street), Rowes were originally in St Pancras and then moved to the site they recently vacated in the Hornet. Cafés and tea-rooms included Kimbells in North Street, the Tudor in East Street, and the Tower in West Street. The Army and Navy stores were known as Morants, and some stores such as Currys, Cover's and Sykes have relocated to new sites and premises away from the city centre. Mention should also be made of the city's cinemas which included the Granada (the most recent to close in 1980), the Gaumont (which became the former swimming pool in Eastgate Square), and the Odeon in South Street.

We are now accustomed to Sunday trading and late-night shopping, but until recently it was normal practice for Chichester shops to close early on Thursdays. Although out-of-town shopping and shopping on the Internet has meant that it is possible to purchase one's household needs without setting foot in the city centre, the introduction of pedestrianisation probably has done more than anything to save the city as a thriving shopping and commercial centre.

The International Stores in East Street were the first food chain store to open in Chichester towards the end of the 19th century. In 1961 J. Sainsbury opened their first supermarket in the country to stock non-food lines and in 1985 they also led the way by opening the city's first out-of-town superstore at Portfield. In December 1993 the store (above) was destroyed by fire but was reopened after being rebuilt in 1994.

In 1964 Sharp Garland's grocery store (shown above; founded in 1665 and claimed to be the oldest in the country) closed and the building was controversially demolished.

C.C. Allen the jewellers in South Street closed in 1986. Mr Ronald Allen and his sister Maisie, seen here shortly before the shop closed, were the owners, and had run the shop for many years, having inherited it from their father. The shop had never been modernised. Latterly they continued business, often behind locked doors and shuttered windows.

Waterstones bookshop now occupies part of the former Dolphin and Anchor Hotel, which closed in 1997. It is thought that the building stands on part of the site of the Roman forum. The Dolphin and the Anchor were originally two inns competing against each other for business, particularly during the heyday of stage coaching at the turn of the 19th century. The Dolphin was also a venue for cock fighting at this time. The two inns amalgamated in 1910.

At the beginning of the 17th century a thriving needlemaking industry was centred on the eastern suburb of St Pancras. Much of this area was destroyed during the English Civil War and the industry never fully recovered, although it survived in a small way until well into the 18th century. Its decline is equally attributable to the increased and cheaper competition from other parts of the country. Today this busy ring road and a terrace of flats serve as a reminder of this once-flourishing cottage industry. In the background can be seen Cover's former shop premises, which were converted into private apartments during the late 1990s.

Sir Laurence Olivier (centre foreground), the Festival Theatre's first director with the theatre's founder Leslie Evershed-Martin (standing foreground, in profile) at the 'topping out' ceremony.

A decision on whether the South Downs are to be designated as a National Park is currently awaited. However, their designation along with Chichester Harbour as Areas of Outstanding Natural Beauty in the mid 1960s has not only helped to ensure their conservation, but also their use and enjoyment by many people for recreational purposes.

Shortly after the Second World War, Dr Thomas Sharp highlighted 'the special character' of Chichester, and more recently Alec Clifton-Taylor described Chichester as 'small and compact, it is an almost perfect place to live and work'. As we look to the future, it is therefore appropriate to conclude with the sentiments of Bernard Price, who did so much to record and capture the spirit of Chichester in recent years through his writings and broadcasting. 'So Chichester moves on, hopefully, as I trust it always will, changing, and being guided by people who love her.'

The remains of the Roman Palace at Fishbourne were discovered by accident during the digging of a water main trench in 1960. The exposed wall foundations clearly indicated that an extremely large building had once stood there, while the pottery fragments showed that it was a surprisingly early Roman date. This revelation led to the organisation of nine seasons of excavations on the site, directed by Barry Cunliffe and manned by over a thousand volunteers, ranging from inhabitants of the village to enthusiastic amateur archaeologists from all over the world. The picture shows the famous 'Cupid on a Dolphin' mosaic soon after its discovery.

Chichester Harbour and the tidal mill at Birdham at the turn of the 20th century.

During the final years of the 20th century the district has experienced major storms and floods. As global warming has taken its effect on the world's weather, hard winters such as those of 1947 and 1962–63 remain only as memories.

In the early hours of Friday, 16th October 1987, a devastating storm, which has since been referred to as a 'hurricane', devastated the counties of south-east England. Thousands of trees were destroyed in its wake, such as those in The Avenue, Chichester, as wind speeds in excess of 100 mph were recorded. As well as considerable damage being caused to buildings, caravans and vehicles. Many homes had to endure several days without electricity while felled power lines were restored.

Another major storm hit the south coast in January 1990 and on 7th January 1998 a tornado or 'twister' devastated Selsey affecting a thousand homes by ripping off roofs (see picture) and was preceded by a 'spectacular thunderstorm and hailstones the size of golf balls'.

During January 1994, Chichester and the River Lavant became the focus of media attention. Exceptionally heavy autumn and winter rainfall caused the tiny river to burst its banks, in contrast to recent years when it failed to flow due to drought conditions.

Described by the National Rivers Authority as 'a one in 200 year event', surrounding villages and the eastern side of the city experienced some of the worst recorded flooding in their history. The village pond in East Dean and a further spring further down the valley at Singleton are the natural collecting points for the spring water that feeds the Lavant. This small seasonal stream takes its name from the word 'levant' or 'lavant', meaning 'landspring'. Traditionally, the springs break out in mid February, or earlier during a wet winter. It flows some nine miles southwards, around Chichester, and eventually into the harbour near Apuldram.

CHICHESTER

The west front of the cathedral and bell tower. The Norman cathedral ('the cathedral church of the Holy Trinity') was built on the site of a Saxon church, St Peter's. Building began during the episcopate of Bishop Ralph Luffa (1091–1123), and the east end was dedicated in 1108. The cathedral was severely damaged by fire twice during the 12th century. The second fire occurred in 1187 soon after the church had been consecrated. Reconstruction took place in 1199 and major building work continued throughout the next two centuries.

Chichester has the distinction of having the only surviving detached bell tower or campanile in the country. It dates from the first half of the 15th century and has also been known as Raymond's or Ryman's Tower. The bells are housed in the octagonal lantern at the top of the Tower. Due to its deteriorating condition, a major restoration project costing in excess of one million pounds is planned as part of the cathedral's restoration programme.

A view of the cathedral from the south-east.

The cathedral and city walls from the Westgate fields. The city walls are Roman in origin and date back to the 3rd century. They run for one and a half miles forming an irregular polygon around the city. They were originally built of earth with a facing of flint and mortar, with two ditches beyond them. The walls we see today are medieval, based on the Roman foundation. The last occasion they gave protection to the city inhabitants was during the English Civil War in 1642. The city gates were demolished during the late 18th century and a promenade walk was formed around sections of the walls. A walls walk can still be enjoyed today.

OPPOSITE: A view of the cathedral and St Richard's Walk from the south.

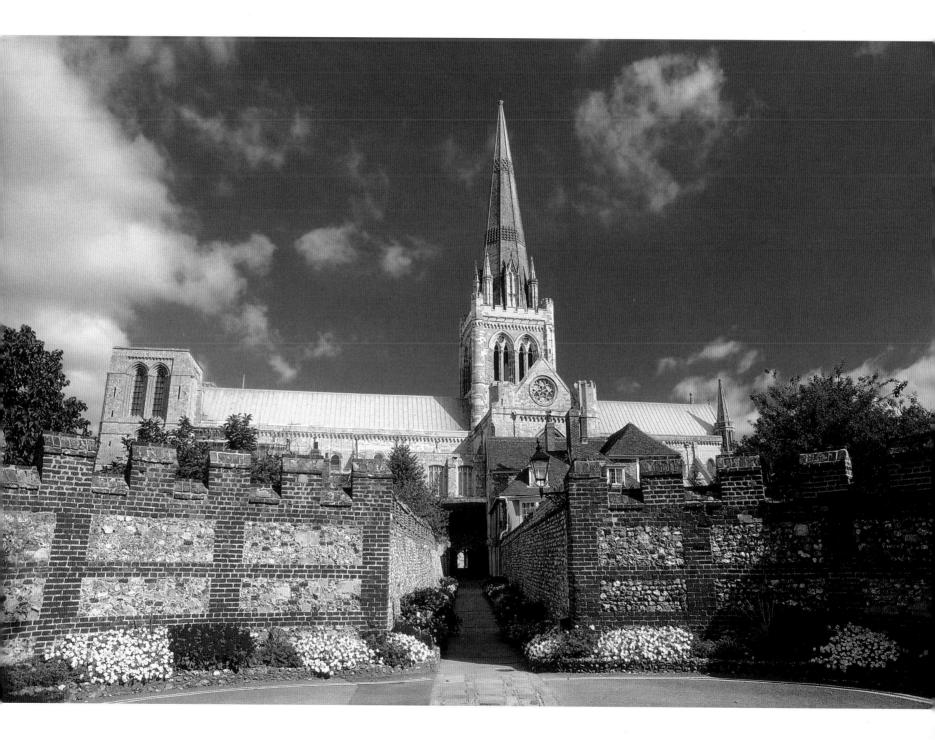

A night-time view of the cathedral from the south-west.

The cathedral precinct, taken from the base of the spire.

The foundation stone of the rebuilt cathedral spire, laid by the sixth Duke of Richmond. The inscription around it reads 'This, the first stone of the spire, was laid by His Grace the Duke of Richmond, May 2nd 1865. Gloria Deo in Excelsis'.

The cathedral spire had collapsed at 1.30 p.m. on Thursday 21st February 1861. The collapse was the result of structural weakness that had been under repair. It happened after a severe storm and it is amazing that none of the workmen was killed. Sir Gilbert Scott was commissioned to rebuild the spire to its original design. The fixing of the weathervane on the newly reconstructed spire took place on 28th June 1866. The spire rises to a height of 84.4 metres (277 feet). The collapse occurred during the reign of Queen Victoria, and so fulfilled a prophecy:

> 'If Chichester church steeple fall,
> In England there's no king at all'

It has so far survived nearly 50 years of another queen's reign.

A view of East Street from the base of the cathedral spire.

Inside the bishop's private chapel is the beautiful circular wall painting of the Virgin and Child, known as the Chichester Roundel. It dates from the mid 13th century and is remarkable for being the earliest known example of English wall painting where the technique of silver-leafing has been used.

The Rt Revd Eric Waldram Kemp, Bishop of Chichester since 1974, at the high altar. He is, at the millennium, the oldest serving bishop in the country. Behind can be seen part of the striking John Piper tapestry installed in 1966.

Part of the magnificent window in the south transept built in the decorative style by John de Langton, bishop from 1305 to 1337. He was Chancellor of England and is buried beneath the window. The stained glass was installed in 1877.

The shrine of St Richard. The original shrine was destroyed during the Reformation in 1538. It is recorded that there were enough jewels, precious stones, rings and silver gilt images taken from it to fill seven chests. The tapestry behind the altar, seen here, is on the site of the shrine in the retro-quire and was designed by Ursula Benker-Shirner and woven at West Dean and in Bavaria.

St Richard is regarded as the patron saint of Sussex. His appointment as Bishop of Chichester in 1245 took place in contentious circumstances, following a dispute with King Henry III who refused to recognise his appointment. As a result his income was withheld and he had to rely on charity for his living for two years, before the king relented. He died in 1253 at Dover and was canonised in 1262. His remains were laid to rest in the shrine in Chichester Cathedral in 1276.

St Richard's Day is celebrated on 3rd April, and it is recorded that the pilgrims who crowded into the cathedral on this day had to be restrained from physically fighting for precedence. The pilgrims, through their offerings, contributed great sums to the cathedral. The traders and innkeepers of the city must also have benefited greatly from their custom.

The late 14th century tomb effigies of Richard Fitzalan and his second wife, Eleanor, the Earl and Countess of Arundel respectively. The monument was rescued from Lewes priory after the Dissolution and was the inspiration for the poem *An Arundel Tomb* by Philip Larkin. The couple are shown expressing their devotion to one another by the holding of hands.

The memorial plaque to Bishop Bell, bishop between 1929 and 1958 is by Mary Gillick. George Bell will be remembered as one of Chichester's most famous bishops. He worked tirelessly for Christian unity, particularly during the Second World War and the conflict with Nazi Germany. He was also a great patron of the arts in the Church, and Gustav Holst (whose ashes are interred in the north transept) performed in the cathedral. T.S. Eliot, Vaughan Williams and the future Indian leader Mohandas Gandhi were just some of the well-known figures who were guests of the Bells and stayed at the Bishop's Palace.

The bust of Bishop William Otter. Bishop Otter College, now University College, Chichester, was founded in 1850, in his memory.

The annual Cathedral Festival of Flowers in May, with its spectacular floral displays is a major fund raising event for the Cathedral Restoration Trust. It is estimated that the planned restoration programme to 2008 will cost in excess of £3 million. In the background of the sailing boat display (above) can be seen the important 12th century carvings depicting the raising of Lazarus, whilst in the more general view of the nave can be seen the Bell–Arundel screen erected in 1961 in memory of Bishop Bell.

A view of the interior and ceiling of the recently completed restoration work to the south-west tower. After the great fire of 1187, the rebuilding of the cathedral was carried out using Jurassic stone quarried from Caen in Normandy. Throughout its history the cathedral has required repair and restoration, particularly in modern times. The Friends of the Cathedral have raised considerable funds towards this work and in 1965 the Cathedral Works Organisation was founded to carry out maintenance and restoration work. The organisation also undertakes work on other historic buildings requiring the expertise of skilled stone masons.

The Bishop Bell tea-rooms and garden provide refreshment to local residents and the many thousands of visitors to the cathedral. It is managed along with the shop in the Bell Tower by Chichester Cathedral Enterprises with the valuable support of volunteers.

'Sculpture in Paradise' is a temporary annual exhibition of contemporary sculpture held during the Chichester Festivities. The exhibition is located in a formal burial ground, known as 'Paradise', which is enclosed by the cathedral cloisters. This selection of photographs shows some of the works exhibited during the 1994–99 Festivities.

The Bishop's Palace is approached from Canon Lane through this gatehouse dating from 1327.

A doorway to a house in the Vicar's Close. The houses in the Vicar's Close date from the 15th century and originally formed part of the College of Vicars Choral. Today, some are the official residences of the cathedral staff whilst others are occupied by people closely associated with the ongoing life of the cathedral. The frontages of the houses on the opposite, eastern side, were reversed in 1825 and they are now facing onto South Street. A wall, which still stands, was built, to separate them from the Close. The remainder of the former Close was demolished in 1831.

The Bishop's Palace gardens are open daily to the public and are managed by Chichester District Council. A local historian, Alexander Hay, described them in about 1725, as having been 'laid out in a plan of great beauty and elegance'.

Conversation piece outside the Deanery, a fine Georgian building, built by Dean Thomas Sherlock in 1725.

For 500 years, Bishop Story's benevolent and visionary gesture to the people of Chichester has been the market cross, acting as the city's focal point, where the four main streets meet. Built like the cathedral of Caen stone it has, over the centuries, received substantial repair and restoration. The bronze bust of Charles I was inserted at the time of the Restoration. The first clock was a gift of a local resident, Dame Elizabeth Farrington, in 1724 'as an hourly memento of her goodwill to this city'. The cross was enclosed with railings when the main produce market was moved in 1808 to the newly erected Butter Market. Its original use having now been declared redundant it was seen by the end of the 19th century as an inconvenience and hindrance to traffic. At the turn of the 20th century there were suggestions that it should be dismantled and removed to a more convenient site. Describing his uncle, Eric Gill, John Skelton draws reference to Gill writing to the *Chichester Observer*, and denouncing this as a preposterous idea.

The cross remained in situ and managed to survive the onslaught of 20th century traffic until relief came during the 1970s with pedestrianisation. A century ago, Joe Faro, or 'Old Joe', was a well-known character on market days selling his pies with cries of 'Pies hot!' from the corner of the cross. Throughout much of the 20th century, until pedestrianisation, a traffic policeman was a familiar figure standing in front of it. Today the cross has become mainly used as a convenient meeting place or a backdrop to busking musicians.

Keith Masters (below) attending to the market cross clock mechanism. A very familiar figure in the city, Keith has lived in Chichester all his life. After leaving school he spent 21 years as a clockmaker before turning to accountancy and then reverting back to his first love of clock making and repairs. He then entered the cathedral as a verger and finally as sacristan. He retires early in 2000 and hopes this will give him more time to enjoy his interest in clocks. His responsibility for maintaining the five city council clocks, including that of the cross, will remain. He remembers that as an apprentice he would visit the cross to help service the clock and later spent fifteen years winding it before electrification of the winding system was introduced in the 1970s. The clock was installed in 1903, as a result of public subscription to commemorate the coronation of Edward VII, and manufactured by Gillett and Johnston of Croydon. It still has a mechanical mechanism and Keith visits the cross once a month to reset the timings, which are often upset by variable weather conditions.

East Street and North
Street are the two principal
shopping streets of the
city. East Street (top left)
has become a popular
venue for pavement artists.

Despite its small size, Chichester is outstandingly rich in architectural heritage and detail. The selection here and on the following page shows just a few of the delights to be found within a comparatively short walk around the city. St John's church (above) which closed in 1976, has recently been restored and voted as one of the country's top 40 most interesting churches.

Further delights and details.

Footscrapers are a reminder of the days in previous centuries when the city streets were not as clean as they are today.

The chapel of St Bartholomew, part of Cawley almshouses.

The Pallants are to be found in the south-east quadrant and reflect in miniature the city's main street plan. The Archbishop of Canterbury held this area as a palatinate throughout the medieval period until 1552 and the name is thought to have derived from it being the Archbishop's Peculiar, or possibly the word 'pale', meaning an enclosed place. Between the 15th and 17th centuries they would appear to have been inhabited by tradesmen and in particular maltsters. There are also references to complaints about the manure left in the streets!

Spershott refers to the Pallants during the early 18th century as 'being very old with few good houses'. The area, like other parts of the city, was transformed during the 18th century and became a highly fashionable place to live. Many of the buildings in the Pallants today have become the offices of accountants, solicitors, surveyors and other professional firms. The 13th century All Saints church in West Pallant is now the headquarters of the local branch of the Red Cross. Nevertheless they still retain their Georgian elegance and are well worth a leisurely stroll through to observe the brickwork, windows, doorways and footscrapers.

OPPOSITE: Pallant House has also been known as Dodo House. The ostriches, the Peckham family crest, sit on top of the gate piers and have been mistakenly referred to as dodos. The expense to which Henry Peckham went in building the house is reflected in the high standard of craftsmanship, both inside and out. Note the finely gauged brickwork and the monogram HP, which can be read both ways by those entering or leaving the house.

When Henry 'Lisbon' Peckham, a young wine merchant built Pallant House in 1712, it cost £3,000 of his wife's £10,000 fortune, an awesome sum at a time when a good town house could be built for about £500. Pallant House was re-opened as an historic house and art gallery in 1982. The faithfully restored rooms and Georgian gardens each reflect a particular period of the house's history. They also provide a lively backdrop for the fine antique furniture, pictures, porcelain and textiles that visitors can discover as they move from room to room, and from the age of Hogarth to the last years of Queen Victoria's reign (below). The 20th century is represented by the gallery's holdings of modern British art from many private collections. Artists represented include Henry Moore, Graham Sutherland, Ben Nicholson, Paul Nash and Barbara Hepworth.

LEFT: The Council House in North Street was designed by Roger Morris and built in 1731. It was paid for by public subscription. An inscribed Roman stone referring to King Togidubnus, discovered nearby in 1723, suggests that the Council House stands close to the site of a Roman temple dedicated to Neptune and Minerva. The stone is now displayed under the portico.

The Assembly Room, which was added in 1783, was designed by James Wyatt. For a short time it became a fashionable venue for balls and it is recorded that dancing would continue until 2 a.m. Work by the Georgian painters, the Smith brothers, George, John and William, is on view. The second Duke of Richmond was a patron and he donated his portrait by William to the City Council. The ante room contains showcases displaying civic insignia, including the mace. Also on show are silver and plate, and royal charters granted to the city.

The City Council and its committees meet in the Council Chamber. The panels around the chamber contain the names of the city's mayors since 1531. Chichester's first recorded mayor was Emery de Rouen in 1239.

RIGHT: The Butter Market was built for the City Corporation in 1807 and opened in January 1808. It was designed by the well-known Regency architect, John Nash. Entered through an imposing portico, it provided covered space for market stall-holders away from the dirty and congested streets. Stall-holders contributed towards the cost of the building by paying tolls on the sale of their produce, which included such items as 'butter, cheese, pickled pork, fowls, cockles and mussels, crabs, dead hogs and turnips'.

LEFT: The Old Theatre in South Street was rebuilt in 1791. It was described as being 'roomy and convenient'. The theatre had been built on the site of an earlier theatre and remained in use until 1850. The building has endured a number of uses, ranging from a brewhouse to a small shopping mall.

RIGHT: The former Corn Exchange is an unlikely location for a McDonald's restaurant. The Corn Exchange was built by George Draper, a local architect, between 1832 and 1833. The main entrance is through a six-column Greek Doric portico.

As a public building, the Exchange was being used for other purposes by the end of the 19th century, notably for theatrical and social functions. It housed the city's last cinema, the Granada, before conversion to a McDonald's.

ABOVE: Considered by the architectural historian Alec Clifton-Taylor to have the most imposing house front in Chichester, Edes House was built by John Edes, a maltster. His wife Hannah completed the building after his death in 1696. The Edes family is connected with Chidham, where John is buried. Their initials can be found in the tympanum over the front door and on some of the rainwater downpipes.

In 1916, West Sussex County Council acquired the property. Having decided to make Chichester the administrative centre for the county it became the County Hall, although various departments had to be located elsewhere in the city. Replaced in the 1930s by the new County Hall built in the former orchard, it became the county library headquarters.

In 1967 Edes House was occupied by the County Record Office, which subsequently moved to new premises in 1989. The house has been extensively restored and is now used by the County Council for meetings as well as for artistic and cultural events.

Apart from historic buildings, Chichester also has a rich variety of more modern architecture. The north-west quadrant of the city in particular, is dominated by the 20th century West Sussex County Council administrative buildings and the circular county library designed by the County Architect F.R. Steele. Included in this selection are details from County Hall, the College of Arts, Science and Technology, the controversial but award-winning Avenue de Chartres car park, the Westgate Centre (opened in 1987 and providing a wide range of indoor leisure facilities) the library, Shippam's paste factory, University College, and Rowes car showroom.

Shippam's of Chichester have long been famous for their pastes and a wishbone sign hangs outside the factory. The business has been based in Chichester for over 200 years. In the 1850s, it employed two assistants and served only the local area. Major production of Shippam's pastes started in 1892 when Charles Shippam set up a factory behind his butcher's shop in East Street. By 1909, 46 men were employed. In 1912 a larger factory was built alongside the East Walls. Since then the factory has been greatly extended. In 1924 the main entrance in East Street was built and in 1953 the large packing building was added. Today, Shippam's main production still takes place on this site within the city walls from where Shippam's products are taken for international distribution. Shippam's remains an important local company employing over 200 people.

During the medieval period, the north-east quadrant was the city's main commercial area containing the priory of the Greyfriars and St Mary's Hospital. The Crooked 'S' alley linking to North Street was bombed during the Second World War. It was also known as the Shambles, after the butchers that once worked there. The area is currently the subject of a redevelopment proposal.

Many of the houses to be found today, particularly in St Martin's Square, Lion Street and Little London, demonstrate the rebuilding that took place in the city during the late 17th and throughout the 18th centuries. St Martin's takes its name from the former church that was demolished in 1906 and is now the site of a small garden.

Among the many interesting aspects of this quarter is the 'Leaping Dolphin' to be seen in St Martin's Street. Carved in wood, it is the work of John Skelton, the sculptor and letterer, who was Eric Gill's nephew and last apprentice. The city museum is located within Little London as is the award-winning Shepherd's tea-rooms.

The interior scene shows St Mary's Hospital. The hospital is hidden behind a row of cottages in St Martin's Square. The building dates from the end of the 13th century. Its external appearance has changed little although over the centuries a number of internal alterations have been made in the interests of residents. The timber-framed aisled hall of the infirmary and chapel is one of the earliest and finest examples of a crown-post collar purlin roof in south-east England. The medieval hospital had few internal walls and the beds would have been arranged along the side walls in the aisles. It would have provided temporary accommodation for travellers and the sick. They were cared for by a small mixed community of brothers and sisters under the custos (or guardian) who was also a priest. At the Reformation, responsibility for the hospital passed to the Dean and Chapter since when they have been trustees of the hospital responsible for its maintenance and administration.

The hospital today is in the charge of a matron. The custos, an Anglican priest, is responsible for worship in the chapel and the pastoral care of the residents. Accommodation for four married couples and eight single persons is provided in the main building and in adjacent cottages. At the heart of life at St Mary's today – as for the past 700 years – is the daily worship in the chapel, which is a condition of residence. The public can view the hospital by appointment with the matron.

Ivy Jerome has been a resident of St Mary's Hospital since 1965. She came from Crawley, but lived previously in Tooting, and still continues to do knitting for charitable causes in India and African countries as well as the new baby unit at Tooting.

Peter Dunnaway outside the family taxi business in Little London, where it has been based since the 1920s. Dunnaways, founded in 1852, is thought to be the world's oldest privately owned carriage company. They are well known for their airport runs, a service that they have been doing since the 1920s when Croydon airport opened.

The staircase in the Ship Hotel. The Ship has interesting military connections and was built by Admiral Sir George Murray as his private house towards the end of the 18th century. Murray, who was born in Chichester in 1759, had a distinguished career, and served under both Sir John Jervis and Horatio Nelson. He led the Fleet at Nelson's victory at the Battle of Copenhagen in 1801. He died in 1819, and the following year 200 dozen bottles of wine were auctioned from the house cellars. There is a memorial to him in the cathedral. The house became the Ship Hotel shortly before the Second World War. General Eisenhower stayed at the hotel in April 1944, and it was here that he met with General Montgomery, Admiral Cunningham and Air Chief Marshal Sir Arthur Tedder, to plan part of the D-Day operations.

In 1591 Queen Elizabeth I visited Chichester and it is alleged that she stayed in a property belonging to John Lumley, Earl of Scarborough. This building, in East Street, is now the Punch House and Lindy Lou luggage shop. The audience chamber in which the Queen met the mayor and citizens of the city is now the shop, and still contains the magnificent Tudor ceiling decorated by Italian craftsmen.

The Punch House was famous for the making and sale of a liqueur known as 'Chichester Milk Punch', which could evidently be drunk at any time of the day. It was a favourite drink of Queen Victoria who, in 1840, appointed the then proprietor, John Hudson, 'to the place of manufacturer of Milk Punch to Her Majesty' by Royal Warrant.

The Chichester wine and spirit business of Arthur Purchase and Son was started in 1780 by the then head of the family. Early records of the business are sketchy and still being researched, but documentary evidence begins with Stephen Purchase born in 1780. He is shown in an 1813 directory as the innkeeper of the Egremont Arms in South Street. It passed to his son Thomas, of the Globe Inn, Southgate, and then in 1868 to Thomas's son Arthur. He moved in about 1910 to the North House Hotel in North Street, where the Old Cross Inn now stands. George, the next in line, moved across the road to 32 North Street, and then in 1956 his son Russell transferred to the present handsome Georgian building at number 31. Russell died in 1970 and was succeeded by his son Christopher, the present head of the firm.

It is believed that the firm is now the oldest surviving wine merchants in the country with an unbroken family history of control. The manager of the shop, Charles Skinner who has worked for the firm for 28 years is seen in the photograph.

The interior of Goodrowes hardware shop in the Hornet. The shop still retains a wonderful, slightly old-fashioned image, its shelves stocked high with all manner of products, none of which is plastic shrinkwrapped in the more modern but frustrating presentation which consumers are having to accept elsewhere.

Goodrowes was formed by D Rowe and Co. in 1943 and particularly specialises in milking and agricultural machinery, in addition to offering a wide range of agricultural services. David Sadler is managing director and the family business also employs David's wife and two sons and includes the County Clothing Shop, which was opened in the 1980s.

Great changes have occurred since the sad decision to close the cattle market was taken in 1990. Today, a trading market takes place every Wednesday and Saturday, and for the remainder of the time the site is devoted to car parking. However, in 1999 it became the venue for the Chichester District Farmers' Market. This market is part of a national movement to provide an attractive alternative to out-of-town shopping, enabling local farmers and small-scale producers of food, drink and crafts to sell directly to the customer. An important criterion is that everything sold must have been produced or grown by the vendor.

The out-of-town shopping park at Portfield to the east of Chichester. The development of this site commenced in 1985 with the construction of a new superstore for Sainsbury's, quickly followed by many more well-known shopping chain stores, some of which moved from the city centre. Despite the huge size of the car park, there are times, particularly at weekends and holiday periods, when not a single parking space can be found.

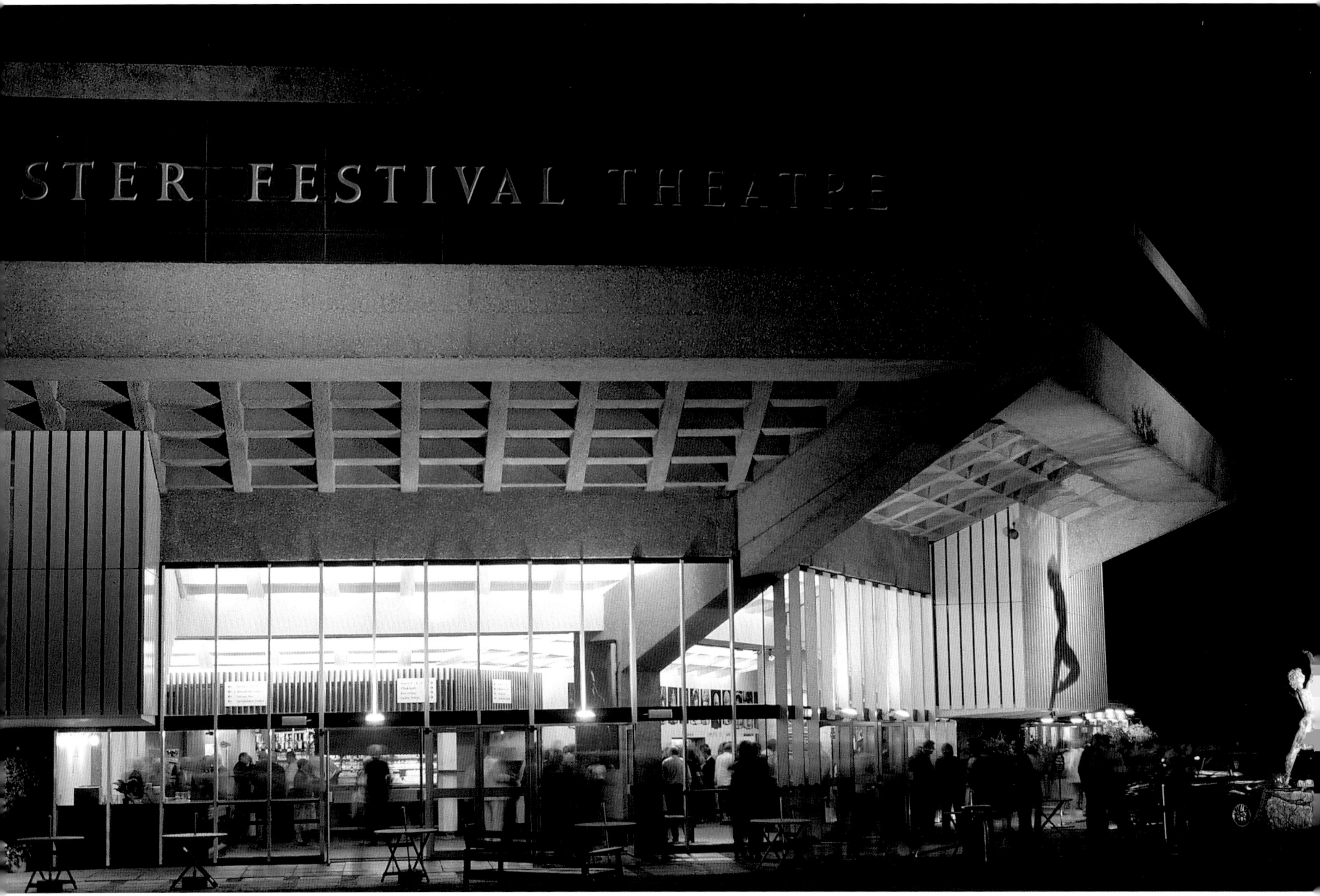
STER FESTIVAL THEATRE

OPPOSITE: The Festival Theatre has maintained an international reputation since its first season in 1962, which was directed by Laurence Olivier. Described as the 'Impossible Theatre' it was founded by Leslie Evershed-Martin, who conceived the idea whilst watching a television programme on a January night in 1959. The programme was about the building of a Shakespeare theatre in the small Canadian town of Stratford, and inspired Leslie Evershed-Martin to establish a theatre in Chichester.

A site was chosen in Oaklands Park and the £105,000 needed to build the theatre, was raised by private fundraising, public subscription and commercial sponsorship. The theatre's running and maintenance costs are still funded from these same sources. The architects, Powell and Moya, broke away from tradition by designing an hexagonal stage with an auditorium containing nearly 1,400 seats, each one being no further than 60 feet away from the stage. Since 1962 a galaxy of theatrical stars including Kenneth Branagh, Julie Christie, Judi Dench, Alec Guinness, John Gielgud, Anthony Hopkins, Derek Jacobi, Penelope Keith, Laurence Olivier, Joan Plowright, Harry Secombe, Omar Sharif, Maggie Smith, Sybil Thorndike and Peter Ustinov have appeared at the Festival Theatre. The adjoining Minerva Theatre was opened in 1989 and during the summer festival season all the productions at the two theatres are original to Chichester, many transferring to the West End. During the winter months, a variety of plays, concerts, ballets, films and a Christmas show take place in the two venues. The Festival Theatre is also a base for one of the country's most prominent youth theatres.

A scene from J.M. Barrie's play, *The Admirable Crichton*, performed in the main theatre in 1997, showing and starring Ian McShane and Victoria Scarborough.

Paul Rogerson has worked for the Festival Theatre for 35 years in various managerial capacities. A much-respected figure in the local community, he has also been involved with the Chichester Festivities since their inception.

The Chichester Festivities. When the decision was taken, in 1975, to stage a three-week Festival of the Arts to celebrate the 900th anniversary of the foundation of Chichester Cathedral, few would have envisaged that 25 years later the annual Chichester Festivities, as it subsequently became, would in turn be celebrating its own Silver Anniversary, not inappropriately in the millennium year.

The intervening period has seen much change, within the Festivities itself, its home city and the wider world (in 1975 for instance the highest ticket price was £2.75, in 1999, £22). One constant, however, has been the Festivities' prime focus on Chichester's magnificent Norman cathedral, its original raison d'être. In latter years, greater use has been made of other locations in the surrounding precinct – the Bishop's Palace for talks and lectures, painting exhibitions in the historic Tudor Room, the cloisters for small-scale exhibitions and notably Paradise, the green sward within the cloisters, for exhibitions of the best in sculpture (see page 31). This last, together with outdoor events on the cathedral green, provides a visible contact between the Festivities and those in the city who may not be drawn to more formal events.

Nearby Goodwood's involvement has also been perennial, at both the splendid ballroom in Goodwood House, and the racecourse, the glorious setting for the Festivities' traditional military tattoo and fireworks spectacular.

Events associated with the Festivities have, at some point in its 25 years, been held in very many other venues. Boxgrove priory and West Dean College gardens outside the city boundaries and St Paul's church, Priory Park (setting for the annual Real Ale and Jazz Festival), the New Park Film Centre and facilities at Chichester's several colleges within the city itself have all been used. Into this last category come a number of venues only newly available during the Festivities' own life span. St John's chapel, in the process of renovation, the restored Edes House in West Street and, most recently, the Minerva Studio Theatre and the venue at the Revelation Warehouse (these last two epitomising a conscious

intention to broaden the Festivities' range and appeal still further, most particularly to the area's young people) are prime examples.

Of all those who have performed at the Festivities over the years, perhaps the following list of 25 gives an indication of both their calibre and diversity – Joan Baez, Janet Baker, Michael Bentine, Judi Dench, James Galway, Lesley Garrett, Evelyn Glennie, Stephanie Grappelli, Roy Hattersley, Jools Holland, Douglas Hurd, Roy Jenkins, Emma Johnson, Nigel Kennedy, Cleo Laine, Jacques Loussier, Yehudi Menuhin, Frank Muir, Michael Parkinson, Sviatoslav Richter, John Simpson, Paul Tortelier, Gillian Weir, Fay Weldon and John Williams. This goes without mentioning numerous leading orchestras, military and brass bands, chamber and vocal ensembles, choirs, speakers and entertainers of national and

international renown, nor the invaluable contributions made both individually and by the very best of our home-grown local talent.

For all that it attracts visitors from outside the area, the Festivities remains first and foremost an integral part of Chichester's own cultural life. It fulfils a vital role in reinforcing Chichester's commercial status and sense of community, whilst simultaneously offering a greatly appreciated opportunity for refreshing and enhancing the lives of its citizens.

Various Festivities including beer barrel races, Children's Day in Oaklands Park, cloisters exhibition, Scottish dancing, and juggling on the cathedral green are shown opposite, whilst the picture above shows the group *Cloud 9* in concert in the cathedral.

The former village school at Westhampnett is now a private house. Surprisingly little is known about the school, but its foundation date of 1839 indicates that it would have been under the patronage of the fifth Duke of Richmond. Its foundation may have been connected with the concern for social improvement at the time. A little further down the road towards Chichester, the parish workhouse was located in Westhampnett Place, which was burnt down in 1899. The workhouse was renowned for its harsh regime. During the 19th century, Westhampnett also had a thriving brickworks, which was located on the opposite side of the road.

Westbourne House School was founded in Folkestone in 1907 and, after evacuation to Devon during the Second World War, was moved to Shopwyke in 1947. The co-educational boarding and day school for children, aged between 3 and 13, at present numbers 290 pupils. It is situated in 25 hectares of parkland.

Shopwyke Park was once the home of the Woods family who rebuilt the present house in 1840. They were related to Gilbert White, the Selborne naturalist. During the Second World War the house was used by RAF Tangmere as an officers' mess and had a lucky escape in 1940 when a Messerschmitt 110 was shot down and crashed in the grounds.

OPPOSITE: The Prebendal School playing cricket on the Westgate fields. The Prebendal is the oldest school in Sussex and its origins probably go back to the time when the cathedral was moved from Selsey to Chichester, during the late 11th century. It was at this time, a 'song school' responsible for housing and teaching choristers. The school was re-founded in 1497 by Bishop Story. The school's name is derived from the Prebend of Highleigh, a canonry, which Bishop Story made into an endowment to fund the school. The school now has nearly 300 boys and girls including those in the pre-prep at Northgate House. Some of its former pupils include William Cawley, Chichester's Member of Parliament, who was one of the regicides who signed Charles I's death warrant. Ironically, another ex-pupil was William Juxon, the chaplain who served Charles I at his execution in 1649. Juxon went on to become Archbishop of Canterbury in 1660 at the restoration of Charles II. Yet another ex-pupil, William Collins (1729–1759), was the son of a Chichester hatter and regarded as probably the city's best-known poet. He led a rather tragic life and is buried in the church of St Andrew-in-the-Oxmarket that is now the Chichester Centre of Arts. An elaborate memorial to him, by John Flaxman, can be found on the south wall of the tapestry in the cathedral.

The Oliver Whitby School, now the Army and Navy department store. The motto *Vis et Sapientia* ('Strength and Wisdom') can still be found over the main entrance door. The building dates from 1904 and replaced an earlier schoolhouse on the site. The school was founded by Oliver Whitby in 1702 'for 12 boys, with a view of qualifying them for especially the sea service'. The school was a Blue Coat school and closed in 1950 when it amalgamated with Christ's Hospital School, near Horsham.

Pupils from the Bishop Luffa C of E School with Chichester MP, Andrew Tyrie, at the opening of the school's new Design and Technology extension in 1999. When the school was opened in 1965 by Queen Elizabeth, the Queen Mother, it was the first Church of England secondary school to be built in Sussex during the 20th century.

Chichester High School for Boys. The Chichester High Schools for Boys and Girls became comprehensive schools in 1971. This followed the amalgamation of the two schools with the Lancastrian Secondary School, which dated back to 1810. The High School for Girls had been founded in 1909 and the High School for Boys in 1928. Year 7 pupils are shown here being taught rugby by their coach, Nick Creaser.

Successful GCSE students of the 1999 academic year at
Chichester High School for Girls with their awards.

The children of the March School, Westhampnett
with the Earl of March. The school is celebrating its
successful fundraising for new school buildings at
the inaugural Goodwood Revival meeting.

New millennium year pupils at St James' School.

The College of Arts, Science and
Technology was opened in 1964 and
currently has over 16,000 students of
which 4,300 are full time, studying a wide
range of academic, commercial, scientific,
technical, recreational and adult
education courses.

University College, Chichester. Formerly
known as Bishop Otter College, it was
founded in 1850 in memory of Bishop
Otter. In 1839 he had established a small
college in Little London for the training
of male teachers. The college
amalgamated with Bognor Regis College
in 1977 to form the West Sussex Institute
of Higher Education. The Institute was
given approval in 1999 to award degrees
and was renamed University College,
Chichester.

The New Park Centre is housed in the former Central Boys School, which was rebuilt in 1887 to accommodate 390 boys. Today, the community association members using the centre include the Chichester Players, an amateur drama group established in 1933, and the New Park Film Centre. The centre is hired for a variety of other uses including martial arts, dog training, toy fairs, auctions and functions, as well as being a meeting venue for the Chichester Camera Club. The future of the building and the surrounding land is uncertain and is currently the subject of a redevelopment proposal.

The Roussillon Barracks have been the home of the Royal Military Police since 1964. The original barracks were built between 1795 and 1813 on the high ground to the north of the city known as the Broyle. Close by is the site where six smugglers were hanged in 1749 for the atrocious murders of a customs house officer, William Galley, and a shoemaker, Daniel Chater. Between 1873 and 1960 the barracks were home to the Royal Sussex Regiment. The Royal Military Police will always be remembered for the annual march they initiated to commemorate their centenary in 1977, celebrated by this statue in front of the keep. A total of over 100,000 soldiers, police and civilians from around the world took part in the Royal Military Police and City of Chichester International March until the last one in 1993. A museum is housed in the keep, which is open to the public, and tells the story of military police history since Tudor times. Military police have been serving in the Balkans throughout the recent troubles and in Kosovo following the 1999 war.

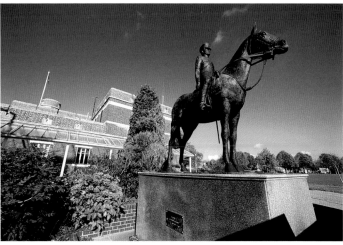

The Mechanical Music and Doll Collection was set up in 1983 in the old Victorian church at Portfield. The fine flint building is an apt location for this array of amazing Victorian artefacts. The owners, Clive and Lester Jones, restore all kinds of mechanical instruments – musical boxes, barrel-pianos, orchestrions, dance organs – and demonstrate them to visitors. Phonographs, early gramophones and over 100 Victorian dolls are also on display. It is a favourite venue for clubs, students and schools in the area who are all fascinated to hear these mechanical music-machines playing as they did years ago. Lester is also producing new versions of the original 'Polyphon' style musical boxes, keeping these skills alive to delight a whole new generation of music lovers.

The staff of the *Observer* series of newspapers outside their premises in Eastgate Square. The newspaper was launched as the *Chichester Observer and West Sussex Recorder* in 1887. It currently holds three prestigious Newspaper Society Awards, including Britain's weekly newspaper of the year. The *Observer* offices occupy the site of the Unicorn Inn, once a favourite watering hole of airmen from RAF Tangmere during the Second World War. The inn belonged to Messrs Henty and Constable and closed in 1960. For a time the building then became the studio of the Festival Theatre before being converted into office accommodation.

Jane Chevis, leader of Chichester District Council at the millennium. The District Council offices are based in East Pallant House, which was extended during the late 1980s to incorporate a new council chamber and additional office accommodation. The original part of the house dates from the mid 18th century and was built by a wealthy resident, Robert Bull, who was also a former mayor of the city.

Born in Chichester, Christopher Doman qualified as a solicitor in 1963. He has spent the whole of his professional life in Chichester with Thomas Eggar Church Adams and its predecessor firms, and now serves as chairman of the partnership. His family had been long-established members of the business community and Christopher has himself always been involved in local activities including Round Table and the Rotary Club of Chichester Priory. He is also company secretary of the Chichester Festival Theatre Trust and the Chichester Festival Theatre Productions company. He was also recently elected as Chairman of Chichester City Centre Partnership Ltd.

The solicitors Thomas Eggar and Son moved to 5 East Pallant in 1936. A succession of mergers during the 1980s and again in 1998 has led to the creation of the present firm of Thomas Eggar Church Adams.

It was at the end of 1981 that Derek and Jacqui Whitby found themselves unemployed. Having searched across the whole of south and south-west England for nearly six months looking for suitable premises to open a photo-retailing business they decided upon Chichester. Since opening their first photo store in Sadler's Walk in 1982, followed by their second shop in East Street in 1986, the business has been a great success story.

Chichester and Chartres – generation after generation. Melissa Cox with her son Henry. The wedding of Melissa's parents, Nigel Purchase from Chichester and Martine Legrand from Chartres, took place in Chartres in 1966 and was the occasion of the first marriage between citizens of Chichester and Chartres. Melissa was born in 1967 making her the first 'twinning' baby, and her son was born in 1999. Melissa's parents live in Chichester marking the continuous link between the two cities.

Chichester and Chartres have been twinned since 1959 and celebrate their 40th anniversary in May 2000. One of Chartres' other twins is Ravenna, near Venice. From friendships formed on visits to Chartres the Chichester/Ravenna twinning developed and the inauguration was celebrated in Ravenna in December 1996 and in Chichester in February 1997.

Henry Barnes cleaning windows in North Street. After a forestry and engineering background, Henry started cleaning windows with his brother-in-law 29 years ago, but soon began to work on his own. He normally starts work about 6.00 a.m., five days a week, with a shorter session on Saturdays. He loves the work and intends to carry on for as long as he is able.

Through his work as an agricultural surveyor, Henry Adams has been a familiar figure in Chichester and with the local farming community for nearly 50 years. He was articled in 1952 to John Gates, then the senior partner of Wyatts. He became much involved with the weekly market selling pigs, poultry and deadstock. Although the market closed in 1990, the sale of deadstock continued until 1998. He became senior partner of Wyatts in 1979 and formed Henry Adams and Partners in 1990, following the take-over of Wyatts by the Prudential in 1987.

Bartholomews (Chichester) Ltd was founded by John Woods Bartholomew, who was the grandfather of Jack Bartholomew, seen here, the present chairman. He opened a shop in North Street during the late 19th century, selling malt and hops for people making their own beer, and also selling hay and horse feed for the large number of horses around at that time. John Woods Bartholomew eventually bought a bicycle and started calling on farmers. This was the beginning of Bartholomews, agricultural merchants.

The business moved to its present site at Portfield between the wars. Today it handles feeds, seeds, fertilisers, crop protection, and crop marketing and deals with many farmers in the south of England. The firm now employs over 200 people and acts as shipping agents and grain exporters, in addition to running a continental road transport business.

In 1819, John Keats and his friend Charles Brown lodged at 11 Hornet Square, now Eastgate Square, the home of an elderly couple, Mr and Mrs Dilke. A contemporary description of the house described it as having 'three airy attics'. It is likely that Keats would have slept in one of these rooms, which is currently occupied by a barber's shop. It was during his time in Chichester that Keats began to write his memorable poem *The Eve of St Agnes*.

Peter Iden (above) and Nigel Purchase are two of Chichester's best known painters. Peter has specialised in watercolour and architectural illustration and, since 1992, in oil painting. Much of his work is inspired by the local Downland landscapes and his exhibitions in the Chichester Centre of Arts are always eagerly awaited. The Centre of Arts is housed in the former medieval church of St Andrew-in-the-Oxmarket. The poet William Collins is buried here, as is John Cawley, three times mayor of the city and father of William Cawley, the regicide and founder of the Cawley Almshouses.

Nigel Purchase owns the Eastgate Gallery and is a member of the Purchase family. He became famous for his commemorative paintings of Chichester, which he started in 1975 at the suggestion of Mervyn Cutten. 1,445 personalities have been included in these paintings. He is currently working with his son Hugo on a painting of surgeons and doctors having a party at Goodwood Racecourse in the company of the Duke and Duchess of Richmond and Lord and Lady March. The painting will be displayed in the new extension to St Richard's Hospital.

A blue plaque marks the site of the house in which Eric Gill, the sculptor, artist and letterer lived at 2 North Walls. The Gill family had moved to Chichester in 1897 when Gill's father enrolled as a student at the Theological College. Gill himself became a student at the Chichester Technical and Art School, and was much influenced by the city's architecture. The cathedral had a major effect on his early life and he married the head verger's daughter. The cathedral contains two pieces of his work, including the memorial to his father-in-law, Henry Moore, which can be seen in the south transept.

St Richard's Hospital was built by West Sussex County Council as a long-stay hospital for the elderly and handicapped. It was opened in August 1939. The hospital became a general hospital during the Second World War under the Emergency Medical Services. In 1948 the Ministry of Health instituted the National Health Service and the Royal West Sussex Hospital and St Richard's Hospital were administered by the Chichester Hospital Management Committee.

The services of the Royal West Sussex Hospital were gradually taken over by St Richard's, resulting in the closure of the Royal West Sussex in 1990. St Richard's is now an NHS trust, known as 'St Richard's Hospital – the Royal West Sussex Trust'. Redevelopment of the hospital began in 1992 and was opened by the Duchess of Gloucester, with the new Accident and Emergency refurbishment scheduled for completion in 2000.

The staff at St Richard's Hospital gather outside the new hospital in 1999 to celebrate being awarded, for the second time, a Whole Hospital Charter Mark – 'the Government's Top Award for excellence in service to the public'.

The Royal West Sussex Hospital has recently been converted into apartments. The hospital was opened as the Chichester Infirmary in 1826. The seventh Duke of Richmond had laid the foundation stone a year earlier. Medical history was made here by John Forbes, Honorary Physician to the infirmary, when he was the first person to use the stethoscope in the country. King George V renamed the infirmary in 1913 as the Royal West Sussex Hospital, in memory of his father, Edward VII. The wisteria growing on the front is claimed to be the oldest in the country. It was planted when the infirmary was built and came from China.

A presentation of Christmas decorations to St Richard's Hospital, that were originally donated to the Chichester Chamber of Commerce. Having stored these decorations at the offices of the *Chichester Observer*, it was felt that the hospital would be a good cause for their usage. Pictured here is St Richard's catering manager Trevor Hayes receiving the decorations from Joyce Tidy of the Chamber of Commerce's commercial committee and Trish Smith of the *Observer*'s promotions department.

Chichester Hospital Radio presenter Paul Morris broadcasting on Channel 11. 'CHR' provides a much-valued service for in-patients at St Richard's. Founded in 1972, it is one of the many voluntary organisations operating in the hospital and broadcasts some 85 hours of hospital radio each week.

Graylingwell Hospital was opened in 1897 as the West Sussex Mental Home, taking its name from the Grayling Well in the grounds. Its water tower, looking from afar like a castle keep, is a prominent feature on the Chichester skyline. The former 18th century farmhouse (left) was once the home of Anna Sewell, the author of *Black Beauty*. The decaying hospital buildings, just over a century later, are no longer suitable for modern mental health care. They present an exciting opportunity for a range of new uses, but their future at the millennium is in the balance and subject to a development plan being drawn up for the site.

OPPOSITE: One of the monthly antique auctions taking place at Stride and Son. The firm was established in 1890 by Charles Stride, and is still today run by a member of the family, Nicholas Stride. From the outset Stride and Son were much involved with local farming and the cattle market, until the latter's closure in 1990. They also handled the great sales of the famous Southdown sheep, when the breed was at its peak before the Second World War. Today, the firm runs a thriving antique saleroom business, as well as estate agency and surveying departments. Charles Stride was also responsible for beginning the development of Summersdale at the start of the 1900s as a planned residential suburb. The Avenue was built for professional people, Highland Road for tradesmen and The Broadway for artisans.

The interior of the chapel of St Bartholomew, part of the hospital known as Cawley almshouses, was built during 1625–26 by William Cawley. The almshouses on either side of the chapel were to house 12 'decayed tradesmen' from Chichester.

William's father John, was three times the city mayor and a major brewer. William born in 1602, carried on the family business and at the age of 25 became the Member of Parliament for Chichester. He later sat for Midhurst and again for Chichester. He supported Cromwell and during the Civil War was an important figure in the area. He was appointed one of the judges at the trial of Charles I, and along with others, became a regicide by signing the king's death warrant in 1649. With the Restoration he had to leave the country. He died in 1666 in Switzerland and it is believed that his son secretly had the body carried home and buried in this chapel.

During the 18th century the hospital was taken over by the City Council as a poor house, and was subsequently enlarged. In the 1920s it became one of a number of workhouses administered by West Sussex County Council. It operated until 1946 when it was taken over by the local health authority and the workhouse closed. In 1999 it was sold to a development company and further changes are therefore likely at the start of the new millennium.

Christmas charity. Councillor Mrs Eva French, the Right Worshipful the Mayor of Chichester and His Grace the Duke of Richmond, the Mayor of the Ancient Corporation of St Pancras, with the Wheelbarrow Club, about to set off from St Pancras church to deliver Christmas parcels to the elderly.

The corporation was founded in 1689 as a show of allegiance to the Protestant succession of William and Mary. Today, it undertakes charity work and the name Wheelbarrow Club is derived from the days when its members had to be 'wheelbarrowed' home from its annual dinner held on 4th November to celebrate the failure of the Gunpowder Plot. Once the parcels have been delivered, the ceremonial procession then returns with the Mayor of Chichester seated in customary fashion in one of the wheelbarrows.

ABOVE LEFT: Members of Selsey Variety Club fund raising in Chichester for St Wilfrid's Hospice new day hospice. Donning Victorian costume for busking sessions, the members are a familiar sight in the city centre. Around £6,000 has been raised by the members for the appeal since April 1999. St Wilfrid's was opened in 1987 for the care of patients suffering from terminal cancer. It is a community-inspired project, built and funded by the generosity of local people and organisations. The day hospice opened in 2000.

LEFT: Phil Spencer – second Vice President of the Rotary Club of Chichester collecting monies at the market cross on behalf of the three Rotary Clubs of Chichester. In their Christmas charity appeal, the Rotary Clubs of Chichester, Chichester Harbour and Chichester Priory spend two and a half weeks collecting money at both the market cross and one of the city's superstores. They aim to raise at least £5,000 annually from this collection alone. All this work is carried out on a voluntary basis, the Rotarians giving their time to the community. The list of charities that have benefited over the years is now considerable.

The Rotary Club of Chichester was formed by a group of city businessmen in 1920 and met for 77 years in the Dolphin and Anchor Hotel until the hotel closed in 1997. They now meet at the equally historic Vicars Hall.

ABOVE RIGHT: Members of the Chichester Singers performing in front of the Christmas tree by the market cross. The Chichester Singers are one of the finest amateur choirs in the south of England. Formed in the late 1950s by the then music adviser to West Sussex County Council, Doris Gould, the choir now has a membership of about 140. Under the direction of Jonathan Wilcox, the current conductor, the choir regularly performs three or four major concerts each year plus several more minor functions. It also performs abroad. Auditions are often held for potential new members, who are recruited from all walks of life and from all parts of the south.

At the start of the 20th century, the writer W.H. Hudson had some disparaging remarks to make about the large number of public houses in the city; there were 50 at the time, and a further 20 beer establishments along with a number of wine and spirit shops. Some interesting names such as the Ship and Lighter, the Fighting Cocks and the King of Prussia are reminiscent of Chichester a century or so ago. Hudson commented that men could be found, 'pipe in mouth and tankard in hand' drinking at 8 a.m. and at closing time, 'a goodly crowd of citizens are seen stumbling forth'.

Westgate House was built in 1751 and a brewery was established on the site in the early 19th century. It became the premises of George Henty and Sons and from 1921 until 1954 Henty and Constable, after the firm amalgamated with S. Constable and Sons.

In 1995 the house became the premises of William M. Mercer, who have since become the largest private sector employer in Chichester with 500 members of staff. The firm (formerly MPA) has been based in Chichester since 1967. Originally sited in what is now known as Metro House at Northgate, the firm expanded into two other offices in the city. William M. Mercer is the world's largest human resource, remuneration and employee benefits consulting firm.

Priory Park became the property of the Duke of Richmond in 1824, and in 1918 the seventh Duke presented it to the city as a war memorial. Cricket was first played in Priory Park in 1851 and Sussex played first-class county cricket here until 1950.

OPPOSITE: An early morning view of the Guildhall in Priory Park. From 1269 to 1538, a priory of the Greyfriars existed on the site of the former Norman castle. After the priory's dissolution, the chancel was converted into a Guildhall, and was also used as a courthouse. In January 1804, the poet and visionary William Blake (writer of the hymn *Jerusalem*) was tried here for sedition. Blake was acquitted. The Guildhall now houses part of the District Museum.

This statue, possibly of a druid, was made by Irene Code and is situated within Priory Park. It formerly stood in South Street and afterwards for many years in a cathedral vault that belonged to Sir William Guy, surgeon, the pupil of John Hunter and friend of Hayley and Flaxman. It was presented to the Priory Park Society by his grandson Dr William Augustus Guy of King's College, London, and erected on the site on 31st May 1873.

Nigel Smith and Andrew Barnes (far right) have been stalwarts of Chichester Priory Park hockey and cricket club sides, having been the only two players to captain both teams. They are also familiar figures in the local community, running their own respective businesses, namely, the estate agents Neal Smith and the sports shop 'Game, Set and Match'. Both were educated at Oakwood School, East Ashling and between them have represented Sussex over 250 times at hockey. The hockey club was founded in 1901, but amalgamated with the cricket club in 1968. It enjoyed its most successful moment when it reached the semi-final of the National Club Knockout Competition in 1998. The year 2001 will be a special year, celebrating the cricket club's 150th anniversary and the hockey club's centenary.

Centurion Way has been created on the route of the former Chichester to Lavant railway line. It is now enjoyed by cyclists and walkers and joins the South Coast Cycle Route. Cycling is now a popular pastime as well as providing an alternative and environmentally friendly method of transport. *Chichester Cycling 2000* is a group dedicated to encouraging cycling in the new millennium. Centurion Way crosses Brandy Hole Lane, once reputedly a haunt of smugglers and also where, at the turn of the 20th century, it had been mooted that a commuter station should be opened to service the expanding Edwardian suburb of Summersdale. The path also possibly crosses the route of the Roman road from Chichester, which led to a local schoolboy suggesting the name Centurion Way.

David Stenning outside the family cycle business, started by his father in 1909.

The stretch of the canal at Hunston is popular with walkers, cyclists and anglers. It was from here that J.M.W. Turner painted his famous view of the cathedral in 1830. During medieval times, Chichester and its harbour were considered to be one of the country's major ports. This is perhaps hard to imagine, as the city itself is not on the sea. The cargoes had to be brought up the harbour to Dell Quay, where they were laboriously transferred into wagons to complete their journey by road. A proposal to connect the city to Dell Quay by canal was first made at the end of the 16th century, but it was not until 1822 that the idea became a reality with the construction of the Portsmouth to Arundel canal. The four and a half mile long section of the Chichester canal was built by John Rennie at a cost of £170,000. It could take vessels of up to 150 tons and the main cargo carried was coal. The canal was never a commercial success and the last cargo was carried to the canal basin in 1906.

The canal is now being developed as a recreational and leisure amenity. The Chichester Canal Society aims to restore through navigation between Chichester and the harbour.

OPPOSITE: Sunset at Southern Leisure Lakeside Village. The former gravel pits adjoining the A27 bypass near Runcton have been developed to provide a variety of leisure facilities including windsurfing, water-skiing, and coarse and trout fishing. The site can accommodate chalets as well as extensive touring camping and caravan pitches.

PETWORTH
AND
MIDHURST

Petworth has grown up in the shadow of its great house and estate, but unlike neighbouring Arundel or, for example, the main Percy stronghold at Alnwick in Northumberland, there is no medieval castle to be seen and the formidable park walls have no towers or turrets. Until comparatively recently the Leconfield estate provided employment, either directly or indirectly, for most of the town and the surrounding villages.

OPPOSITE: The palatial west front of Petworth House was built during the last years of the 17th century as part of the great re-modelling of the house undertaken by the sixth Duke of Somerset, who engaged master craftsmen, such as the wood carver Grinling Gibbons, to work on the house. The 'Proud Duke', as he was nicknamed, had married the heiress Elizabeth Percy, whose ancestors were the Earls of Northumberland and had owned Petworth since 1150. The present building incorporates part of their former castle or fortified house, of which the chapel, built in 1309, survives.

In 1750, the Percy estates were divided and Petworth passed to the sixth Duke's grandson, Charles Wyndham, second Earl of Egremont. During the 1750s, Lancelot 'Capability' Brown landscaped the park. It is considered to be one of his greatest creations and the inspiration for some of J.M.W. Turner's finest paintings.

Charles's son, the third Earl of Egremont, was one of the most remarkable men of his times. During his earldom, which ran for nearly three quarters of a century, Petworth enjoyed what has been described as its golden age. The earl was a patron of the arts, agriculture and social improvement. He also financed local canal projects and was famous for his hospitality. On the estate he built Stag Park, the magnificent model farmstead, and organised the vaccination of Petworth residents by Dr Jenner against smallpox.

Petworth passed to the earl's natural son, who was created Lord Leconfield. The sixth Lord Leconfield was created the first Lord Egremont; and although the house and park were given to the National Trust shortly after the Second World War, the second Lord Egremont and his family still live in the house.

The annual kite festival attracts kite enthusiasts from all over southern England. It is traditionally the opening event of the Petworth Festival, which was founded in 1979 for the artistic and cultural enjoyment of the local community.

Open-air concerts with fireworks have been organised annually by the National Trust in Petworth Park since 1987. Three nights of popular and classical music attract a total audience in the region of 20,000 people.

OPPOSITE: The house, seen from the west across the landscaped park. The hillside to the left and the lake in the foreground form part of the 'Capability' Brown landscape. The lake covers the site of a series of rectangular fishponds, and a stable block demolished in 1720 stood not far from the front of the house.

Food historian Peter Brears and colleagues are seen here dressed as Victorian chefs in the restored kitchens of Petworth House. At the end of the 19th century there were 35 staff employed in the house alone under the control of the house steward. A roasting chef and a pastry chef, who were usually French, assisted the chef.

Cobbett described Petworth on his visit in 1823 as 'a nice market town, but solid and clean'. Cobbett would have only experienced horse traffic, but cars and lorries have plagued the town's narrow and winding streets for decades now. The streets are, however, a delight to walk around and reveal an abundance of local vernacular styles and materials, with some delightful small gardens just visible behind walls and gates. Former timber-framed buildings have often been concealed by a later stone or brick façade. The cobbled Lombard Street is closed to traffic and leads from the Square towards St Mary's church. The church has no spire now, but an earlier one had led to the verse 'Proud Petworth, Poor People; High Church, Crooked Steeple'. A new spire, designed by Sir Charles Barry was originally intended for a Brighton church. It was erected in 1827, but it was taken down in 1947 (see the Introduction section). In addition to Petworth House, the Cottage Museum, the Doll House Museum, and the many antique shops make Petworth a fascinating place to explore.

Petworth Leconfield Hall was built in 1794 as the Petworth Town Hall. It is now used for general public and community purposes and during 1999 was restored and refurbished.

Petworth has established itself today as one of Southern England's leading centres for antiques. Shown on these pages is an interior of the Petworth antique market and a small selection of antique shop windows.

Peter Jerrome, local historian and chairman of the Trustees of the Petworth Cottage Museum. In association with Jonathan Newdick he is well known for his books about the work of the famous Petworth photographer, George Garland.

The sitting room in the Petworth Cottage Museum. The museum was opened in 1996 and is a reconstruction of how 346 High Street, a Leconfield estate worker's cottage, may have appeared in 1910, at the end of the Edwardian era. Mrs Mary Cummings, a seamstress at Petworth House, occupied the cottage between 1910 and 1930. The cottage reconstruction has been a community project and is run as a charitable trust with volunteer helpers and a Friends organisation to assist with fundraising.

OPPOSITE: Daintrey House is a particularly impressive Georgian house in the centre of the town, with an intricate iron railing garden fence in front.

Prisoners' graffiti on a wall by the police station is an eerie reminder of the House of Correction, which was built in 1778 and demolished just over a century later. An austere and severe regime was operated, and punishments included solitary confinement and hard labour on a treadwheel monitored by a device called an 'ergometer', which measured the daily amount of energy each prisoner discharged over a three-month period. The Petworth Society magazine recounts that the diet prescribed by the prison governor was 'seven ounces of the best wheaten flour boiled in water so as to make a quart of thick gruel or rather hasty pudding and seasoned with salt for breakfast, and one and a half pounds of the best wheaten bread daily'.

When granted his new estates after the Conquest, Roger de Montgomery recognised not only the strategic importance of Midhurst, but also its commercial potential. The town was planned around a market place and a chapel (the predecessor of the parish church of St Mary Magdalene and St Denys), within the outer bailey of the castle on St Anne's Hill and identifiable today as the area around Sheep Lane and Church Hill. As the town grew and the number of burgages, or house plots let to tradesmen, increased, a second market place was founded by the Knights Hospitallers, which is now the triangular plot of land bordered by Rumbolds Hill, Wool Lane and West Street. By the end of the 16th century, a third market place had been developed along the north-east side of North Street.

A timber castle may have been built by Roger de Montgomery after the Conquest, although his successors as Lords of the Manor, Savaric Fitzcane and then the de Bohun family, have been credited with its development. The de Bohuns abandoned the site sometime during the late 13th century in favour of 'La Coudraie', a name meaning a hazel wood, which it is thought was located on or in the vicinity of the present Cowdray ruins, where they built a moated manor house. This view shows the remains of the castle foundations on St Anne's Hill.

OPPOSITE: Midhurst, like Petworth, has a traffic problem. Fortuitously larger vehicles have been diverted away from the narrow streets of the original town below the castle foundations on St Anne's Hill. Here it is possible to trace the development of the town through its variety of traditional buildings ranging from 16th and 17th century timber framing to elegant Georgian brick and local stone buildings.

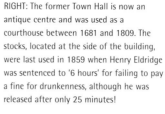

RIGHT: The former Town Hall is now an antique centre and was used as a courthouse between 1681 and 1809. The stocks, located at the side of the building, were last used in 1859 when Henry Eldridge was sentenced to '6 hours' for failing to pay a fine for drunkenness, although he was released after only 25 minutes!

The well-known Spread Eagle Hotel claims to date from 1430, but the building was added to in the 17th century.

South Pond with its ducks and wildfowl, is a picturesque landmark and public amenity on the southern edge of the town. The pond was originally created as a millpond for the former mill on the other side of the road. A stream links the pond with the River Rother; and, a wharf was constructed alongside it in the late 18th century to service the Rother Navigation.

ABOVE: The public library at the top of the intriguingly named Knockhundred Row has been converted from four timber-framed cottages. It stands just outside the position of the former northern entrance gate to the original town.

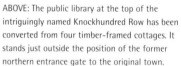

The famous science fiction writer H.G. Wells has a number of interesting links with Midhurst. The town and surrounding area were the inspiration for some of his books, including The Invisible Man. He spent much of his childhood at Uppark where his mother was housekeeper.

ABOVE RIGHT: The Tudor Market Hall would possibly have originally resembled the one from Titchfield, which has been re-erected at the Weald and Downland Open Air Museum. In 1672, the upper chamber became the schoolroom for the newly founded Grammar School. The school was founded by Gilbert Hannam, a coverlet maker, who had bequeathed £20 per annum for the educating of 12 poor children 'in Latin and Greek, and in Writing and Arithmetic, if they be capable to learn . . . ' . The fortunes of the school declined and it was forced to close in 1859, but it was re-founded in 1881.

The last surviving burgage stone, which would have been attached to a burgage house.

A cottage in neighbouring Easebourne belonging to the Cowdray estate, identifiable by the distinctive Cowdray yellow paintwork.

The A272 through Cowdray Park was once gated by Benbow Pond and opposite the priory church in Easebourne in order to contain the deer herd. As the number of motor vehicles increased during the early years of the 20th century, the 'byepass bridge' was constructed and remained in operation until the Second World War.

The priory of St Mary at Easebourne was founded in the early 13th century and incorporated the existing parish church. The prioresses appear to have gained a reputation for their extravagances and the nuns were once described as 'wild females'. A side door in the church leads to the former cloister, which now forms the vicarage and other private homes. A grand monument to Sir Anthony Browne (the first Viscount Montague of Cowdray) and his two wives was moved here from Midhurst church during the 19th century.

The chemist shop, D. Morton-Hickson in Church Hill, still retains a wonderful old-fashioned interior, and it was here that the young H.G. Wells was apprenticed to the chemist, Mr Colap. During his short time in the shop he was sent to the recently re-founded Midhurst Grammar School to learn Latin in order to understand prescriptions. His time in the shop was to be the inspiration for his novel *Tono-Bungay*. In 1883 he returned to the Grammar School as a pupil-teacher. At this time he took lodgings above what is now Ye Olde Tea Shoppe in North Street. David Morton-Hickson is shown at the counter whilst behind can be seen the 'prescriptions prepared' sign, one of several signs within the shop that he has restored.

A view of the kitchen in the Cowdray ruins. Ironically it is the one part of the original house not to have been destroyed by the fire, when so often the kitchen was the source of fire in many large houses. Charcoal stoves can be seen in the foreground of the photograph.

The dramatic ruins of Cowdray House are the result of a disastrous fire that gutted this great Tudor house in September 1793. Descriptions and engravings are able to reveal something of the scale and grandeur of the building and its contents. If it had survived, it would today undoubtedly be considered as one of the finest examples of its kind in the country. The house was begun by Sir David Owen in about 1520 and largely completed by his successor, Sir William Fitzwilliam, who became the Earl of Southampton.

Cowdray was inherited by the Earl of Southampton's half-brother, Sir Anthony Browne in 1542. Browne enjoyed royal favour despite being a Catholic, and had been granted the Battle Abbey estate after its dissolution by Henry VIII. It was here that the more well-known version of the Cowdray curse was made, when a monk allegedly told Browne that his house and family would perish by fire and water. The curse, however, took 250 years to be fulfilled. Browne's son became the first Viscount Montague and his descendant, the eighth Viscount – and last of the line – died in a drowning accident on the River Rhine, almost immediately after the fire in 1793.

Both Edward VI and Queen Elizabeth I were lavishly entertained at Cowdray, notably the latter who stayed for six days in 1591. It is recorded that she shot buck with a bow and arrow, and that three oxen and 140 geese were prepared for one day's breakfast. Guy Fawkes was a manservant to the second Viscount Montague and as a result he was implicated as being a conspirator in the Gunpowder Plot. This resulted in Montague being fined and imprisoned in the Tower of London for a year.

During the 19th century the burnt-out shell became a 'Romantic' ruin attracting the attention of tourists and artists, including Turner and Constable.

In 1908, the Cowdray Estate was purchased by Sir Weetman Pearson, later the first Viscount Cowdray, who set about preserving the ivy-clad ruins. The present fourth Viscount inherited the estate in 1995 and there are future plans in the new millennium to preserve and make the ruins more accessible as a visitor attraction.

The game of polo has become synonymous with Cowdray Park, where it has been played since 1910. Polo is considered to be one of the oldest recorded games in the world. It has been a favourite pastime of royalty, most notably the Prince of Wales, who has frequently played at Cowdray. Gold Cup Day shown here is the highlight of the Cowdray polo season.

THE
COUNTRYSIDE

OPPOSITE: On the South Downs above Upwaltham looking east.

A view looking south across the Chichester district from Blackdown, the high sandstone ridge near to the district and county border. Rising to a height of 280 metres (918 feet), it is the highest point in Sussex. Tennyson lived the latter part of his life at Aldworth, the house he built near Lurgashall not far from Blackdown.

Traditional harvesting at Oving, where the wheat has been grown for thatching purposes. At the new millennium, the countryside and rural life is under threat as farmers face economic difficulties and change, due to factors such as the BSE crisis and the decline in the number of milking herds.

Although Richard Cobden lies buried in neighbouring West Lavington churchyard, it is with Heyshott that he is more commonly associated. Born in 1804 at Dunford Farm, Cobden became a successful businessman and travelled extensively before entering Parliament in 1841. In a decade often referred to as the 'Hungry Forties', he became the leader of the Anti-Corn Law League and a national hero when the Corn Laws were repealed in 1845. In 1847 he re-purchased the former family home at Dunford, with the help of a public donation for his work, and he set about building a new house. Dunford today is used as a conference centre and belongs to the YMCA. Cobden died in 1865 and a tablet was erected by his daughter and son-in-law above his pew in St James' church, Heyshott.

Due to the long hours of sunshine and quality of light, many nurseries are sited on the Chichester plain. The Hazlewood VHB Runcton nursery contains nearly 14 hectares of glasshouses, including the UK's largest glasshouse, which covers an area of nearly 10 hectares alone. An estimated 100 million tomatoes are grown in this glasshouse and in all half a million tomato plants are grown on the site.

Donaldson's Flowers are the largest UK-owned cut-flower producer, growing on average 10 million chrysanthemum stems throughout the year, of which approximately one third are supplied to Sainsbury's supermarkets.

Modern farming methods and unusual crops are found on the coastal plain. The picture here of maize planting at South Mundham gives an almost surreal quality to the landscape.

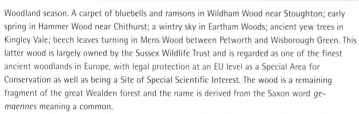

Woodland season. A carpet of bluebells and ramsons in Wildham Wood near Stoughton; early spring in Hammer Wood near Chithurst; a wintry sky in Eartham Woods; ancient yew trees in Kingley Vale; beech leaves turning in Mens Wood between Petworth and Wisborough Green. This latter wood is largely owned by the Sussex Wildlife Trust and is regarded as one of the finest ancient woodlands in Europe, with legal protection at an EU level as a Special Area for Conservation as well as being a Site of Special Scientific Interest. The wood is a remaining fragment of the great Wealden forest and the name is derived from the Saxon word *ge-maennes* meaning a common.

Kingley Vale is a national nature reserve managed by English Nature and is located four miles north-west of Chichester. It is famous for its great yew forest, which was probably first planted 500 years ago. A few of these ancient yews remain, but most of the trees are between 50 and 250 years old. At the start of the 1900s, the writer E.V. Lucas wrote 'Kingley Vale, always grave and silent, is transformed at dusk into a sinister and fantastic forest, the home for witchcraft and unquiet spirits.' In the reserve, evidence exists of a wide range of archaeological remains as well as a great number of different plants, birds, mammals and insects.

Village and country churches. The church is the one building to have silently witnessed all the changes around it, in many cases throughout the last entire millennium.

St Andrew's, Didling has been romantically christened the 'shepherds' church'. Its simple interior still contains medieval pews and a large and aged yew guards the churchyard. The sound of sheep bells can sadly no longer be heard, but sheep still graze the surrounding Downland pastures.

The hamlets of Racton and Lordington are better known for the families who have lived there. The church at Racton houses monuments to the Gounter family. Sir George Gounter assisted the future King Charles II in his dramatic escape from Cromwell's troops after the Battle of Worcester in 1651.

Burton Park, the former St Michael's girls' school, along with other buildings in the park, has been converted into private apartments and houses, thus creating a community for the church to serve once again. The present mansion was built in 1831 on the site of an earlier house. Burton was once a medieval village and the diminutive church is its only survivor. Described by Nairn and Pevsner as 'one of the mellowest in Sussex', the untouched interior contains not only wall paintings, but also monuments and brasses to the Goring family.

RIGHT: The 13th century church of St Michael, situated in the remote Downland hamlet of Up Marden. It was described by Nairn and Pevsner as having 'one of the loveliest interiors in England'.

The Benedictine priory of Boxgrove is one of the county's most important ecclesiastical buildings. The priory was founded in the early 12th century and was dissolved by King Henry VIII in 1537, leaving only the priory church for the villagers to worship in. The parish church of St Mary and St Blaise contains a vaulted ceiling in the chancel, painted during the mid 16th century by Lambert Barnard, and the elaborate de la Warr chantry chapel. Completed just before the Dissolution, the chantry remains empty as its builder, Lord Thomas de la Warr of Halnaker, could not be buried there because of the Reformation.

St Mary the Virgin, Upwaltham in winter snow. Cardinal Manning, who was once curate to the rector at nearby Graffham, wrote 'The Hills . . . Upwaltham Church . . . the Downs seem to me only less beautiful than Heaven'. William Cobbett travelled through Upwaltham on one of his Rural Rides in 1823. Cobbett described the parson, a man called Tripp, as 'an impudent fellow' because he had referred to the parsonage as 'a miserable cottage'.

The countryside around the Mardens and Stoughton is probably one of the remotest parts of the South Downs. St Mary's, Stoughton is considered to be late Saxon in origin. The church contains the tomb of Sir Geoffrey Pole, who lived at neighbouring Lordington. His family suffered dreadfully at the hands of Henry VIII. His aged mother, the Countess of Salisbury, and one brother were beheaded. The Countess was imprisoned briefly at Cowdray before her brutal execution, but her other son, Cardinal Pole, survived to become Archbishop of Canterbury during Queen Mary's reign.

St Mary's, Bepton. The church was described by the historian James Dallaway as having 'nothing to distinguish it from the very simple architecture of those in the district'. It stands in a secluded spot above a pond and in its graveyard were buried victims of the Black Death. Inside the church can be found a tomb to a 14th century Norman with a Scandinavian name, a man who is thought to have been seven foot tall. The hamlets of Bepton, Didling and Treyford together with the deserted settlement of Linch, lie along the escarpment of the Downs and it is extraordinary to think that they all supported their own churches, Treyford even having two churches, both of which have now been destroyed.

The tiny 12th century Downland church of St Mary at North Marden, is one of four Sussex churches still retaining its original simple plan with a rounded chancel or apse.

St Mary's, Chithurst stands on a knoll in a tranquil position above the River Rother. This tiny and simplest of churches has probably changed little over the last millennium. The collection of worn and leaning gravestones in the churchyard makes a picturesque site and some slabs are claimed to be nearly as old as the church. The church pamphlet mentions that in 1956 the church was threatened with closure when the Rector of Iping reported that only one person now attended the monthly service. Happily the threat of redundancy did not materialise and the church became a chapelry of Trotton.

An unusually worded headstone in Bosham churchyard to Thomas Barrow which shows him falling from his sloop *Two Brothers*. A 'horse' in a definition of 1711, was a convenience for the men to tread on, in going out to furl or unfurl the sails.

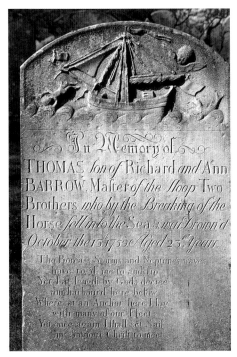

This unusual headstone is to be found in the east wall of East Dean church and belongs to William Peachey, the village blacksmith, who died in 1688. He fought in the Civil War for the famous Roundhead troop known as the Hambledon Boys. Peachey made broadswords for the troop, which were inscribed with their owners' names and motifs. The swords were reputedly buried with their owners. Note the spelling and broken wording.

ABOVE: The chancel wall of St Peter's church at Westhampnett contains re-used Roman bricks, laid in herringbone fashion and dating from the late Saxon period. The churchyard also contains the tombs of three Bishops of Chichester.

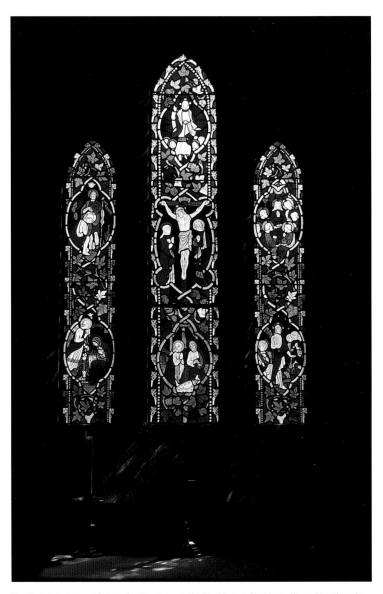

The Victorian rector of Selham for 57 years was the Revd Robert Blackburn. He could perhaps be described as a 'squarson'. He was responsible for installing the stained glass windows in the 11th century church. He was immensely proud that his wife could trace her ancestry back to the Plantaganets. As a result the windows include his children's heraldic shields. When the sun shines through, the windows have been described as having a 'jewel-like quality' because of the intensity of the various colours incorporated.

Donnington church on the coastal plain surrounded by open skies and wind-blown fields. The chancel has been described as a perfect specimen of 13th century architecture, and the nave is separated from the aisles by arches of the same age. A window in memory of Edward VII has a figure of an angel bearing the message of peace and goodwill.

St George's, Trotton is famous for its magnificent medieval brasses and wall paintings. It contains the earliest known brass of a woman, Margaret Camoys, seen here, dating from 1310. Trotton's other famous brass is of Thomas, Lord Camoys, a hero of Agincourt and his wife, Elizabeth, the widow of Sir Henry Percy, immortalised by Shakespeare as Harry 'Hotspur'. An image of their brass has been embroidered on one of the colourful collection of kneelers.

OPPOSITE: A popular view from Harting Downs of South Harting, with its church spire and the Hampshire border beyond. The area of Downland is owned by the National Trust and is a designated Site of Special Scientific Interest. When visited a century ago by W.H. Hudson, he paid South Harting the compliment of considering it to be the most attractive of all Downland villages. Apart from its proximity to Uppark, the village's other claim to recognition is having been the home, for a short time, to the author Anthony Trollope. Many of the older buildings around the Hartings are constructed with the distinctive local chalky white clunch stone.

ABOVE: Shulbrede Priory, near Linchmere on the northern boundary of the district with Surrey. The priory was founded at around the turn of the 13th century for five canons of the Augustinian order. After the Dissolution it became a farm and at the beginning of the 20th century it was converted into a private home by the MP Arthur Ponsonby and his wife Dorothea, the daughter of the composer Sir Hubert Parry. The 19th century historian, James Dallaway makes reference to some 'rude' frescoes in the prior's lodging, but he could not have been referring to the delightful animal nativity scene announcing, in Latin, the birth of Christ in Bethlehem.

CENTRE: The district contains many examples of large country houses and manor houses. Rymans at Apuldram is a small manor house built by William Ryman during the early 15th century. An unfounded story claims that Ryman had intended to fortify his new home, but when refused permission, the surplus stone was acquired by the Bishop of Chichester, who used it for building the bell tower. Apuldram is a shrunken medieval village, at the edge of Chichester Harbour near Dell Quay. During the Second World War it had an airfield which played its part in the D-Day landings. Today the hamlet is best known for Apuldram Roses, a specialist rose nursery.

RIGHT: Cakeham Manor, West Wittering was a residence of the Bishops of Chichester, and a favourite one of Bishop Sherburne who added the hexagonal brick lookout tower at the beginning of the 16th century.

Eartham House, now Great Ballard School, was designed by Edward Lutyens in the early 1900s. It stands on the site of an earlier house owned by William Hayley, the poet, between 1774 and 1800. Famous visitors to Eartham at this time included the historian, Edward Gibbon, the poet William Cowper, and the artist, Romney. William Huskisson bought the house from Hayley and there is a tablet to him in the village church. He was a former Member of Parliament for Chichester who has the misfortune to be remembered as the first person to die in a railway accident. In 1830, as President of the Board of Trade, he was attending the opening of the Manchester to Liverpool line, when he was accidentally run over by George Stephenson's *Rocket*. There are monuments in the church to William Hayley's son, Thomas, carved by John Flaxman, and to Sir John Peniston Milbanke, who lived at the house. Sir John won the Victoria Cross in 1900 during the Boer War, but was killed at Gallipoli in August 1915.

Lavington Park, which became Seaford College after the Second World War, was built at the end of the 18th century by John Sargent, close to the site of the original Elizabethan house. In 1807 Sargent's brother George, a captain in the 9th Regiment of Foot, was shot by a deserter from his regiment who was hiding in nearby Charlton Forest. A beech tree, now known as Captain Sargent's tree, still stands in the forest where the murder took place. Two of John Sargent's daughters married future eminent 19th century churchmen, namely, Samuel Wilberforce, son of William the anti-slavery campaigner, who became a bishop (and acquired the nickname 'Soapy Sam') and Edward Manning, who became a cardinal. The Wilberforce family inherited Lavington Park as a result of the marriage.

LEFT: Set in 700 hectares of parkland on the edge of the South Downs and some three miles north of Emsworth, Stansted Park is one of the most elegant stately homes in southern England. Stansted was originally a royal hunting lodge. It was destroyed during the Civil War except for the chapel. Another house was built by William Talman, the architect of Uppark, for Richard Lumley, later first Earl of Scarborough, in 1686. This building was burnt down in 1900 and rebuilt in 1903. Home to the Earls of Bessborough from 1925 to the death of the tenth Earl in 1993, it is now owned by the Stansted Park Foundation, a charitable trust dedicated to the protection of the estate in perpetuity for the nation.

The house displays extensive family portraiture, furniture, tapestries and porcelain. The 'Below Stairs Experience' takes the visitor through a veritable warren of servants' rooms that one rarely gets to see in a stately home, including the butler's quarters, the footmen's bedrooms, wine cellar, the crypt, servants' hall, housekeeper's rooms and the old kitchen.

The ancient chapel was restored in 1819 and adjoins the Bessborough Arboretum. The east window was a source of inspiration to John Keats when writing *The Eve of Saint Mark*. The estate at that time belonged to Lewis Way who attempted to transform Stansted into a college for the conversion of Jews. The extensive walled gardens include the Stansted Park garden centre and Ivan Hick's surrealist 'Garden in Mind'. Cricket is played on the cricket ground in front of the house most Sundays through the summer months.

OPPOSITE ABOVE: The Vandalian Tower on the Uppark estate is a folly, captured here in a dark and mysterious light. Named after an abortive American colony project, the folly was designed by Henry Keene for Sir Matthew Fetherstonhaugh in 1773 although not completed until after his death in 1776. It was used as a pleasure house by Sir Harry Fetherstonhaugh, and it is recorded that diners would have to be wheelbarrowed down the hill after a night of excessive feasting. It became ruinous after a fire in 1842.

OPPOSITE BELOW: Uppark enjoys a commanding position on the Downs above South Harting with spectacular views southwards towards the coast and the Isle of Wight. The house has become famous for the disastrous fire that gutted the interior in August 1989, and the remarkable story of its restoration. The original house was built in about 1690 by it is thought, the architect William Talman, for Lord Grey of Wercke (later created Lord Tankerville). In 1747 it was bought by Sir Matthew Fetherstonhaugh who, with his wife, re-modelled and furnished the house in a grand fashion, reflecting their travels on the continent. Their son, Sir Harry, continued to emulate his parents' collections and Repton was engaged to carry out further improvements to the house and park.

Sir Harry's flamboyant lifestyle has become legendary for his liaison with the young Emma Hart (later to gain prominence as Nelson's Lady Hamilton) and for marrying at the age of 70 his 20-year-old dairymaid who, on his death, inherited the estate. The Prince Regent was for a time a regular guest and enjoyed horse racing on the Downs, which it is said he considered to be better entertainment than Newmarket. The interior of the house was to remain comparatively unaltered from the time of Sir Harry's death in 1846. The National Trust who have owned the property since 1954, took the brave decision to return the house to its original condition before the fire. This they achieved with remarkable success using a variety of conservation techniques and traditional craftspeople. The house was re-opened to visitors in 1995.

Binderton House was built by Thomas Smyth in about 1677 and further alterations were made in the 18th century. In the 1940s and early 1950s it was the country home of the former Prime Minister, Sir Anthony Eden. It has now been converted into private apartments.

The ruins of Halnaker House, a medieval mansion with Tudor additions. During the 16th century it was the home of Thomas West, Lord de la Warr, and was visited by King Edward VI in 1551. One of Halnaker's interesting features was a well house, operated by a donkey wheel. The house had become part of the Goodwood estate in 1765, after which it gradually fell into disrepair.

The upper Lavant valley at Binderton. Binderton is the site of a shrunken medieval village. Alongside the busy A286 can be seen an unusual ruined structure which was built by Thomas Smyth as a chapel. Although it was never consecrated, Smyth himself was once buried there. His tomb was removed to West Dean during the 19th century.

Ballooning over the West Sussex countryside. The British School of Ballooning was one of the first balloon companies established in the country offering champagne balloon flights and is based at Ebernoe.

This windmill, which is a prominent local landmark, stands on top of Halnaker Hill, commanding views of the coastal plain below. Part of the track leading to the mill is on the line of Stane Street, the Roman road that crosses the hill. The first reference to a mill was recorded in 1540. The third Duke of Richmond built the present mill for his tenants in about 1780. It fell into disrepair after a lightning strike in 1905. The mill was immortalised in a poem *Ha'nacker Mill* by Hilaire Belloc, who lived at Slindon. The sweep frames were restored in 1934 as a memorial to the wife of Sir William Bird, who lived nearby.

The Weald and Downland Open Air Museum at Singleton, near Chichester, has developed over 30 years from small beginnings to become the leading museum of historic buildings in England. The museum is set in 20 hectares of pasture and woodland with magnificent views deep in the South Downs.

Established in the late 1960s by a small group of enthusiasts led by Storrington historian Dr Roy Armstrong, its mission is to encourage people's interest in the rich heritage of vernacular buildings in south-east England. It has also developed strong collections relating to building crafts and technology and rural life and landscapes. In 1998 the national importance of its work was recognised when the Government accorded the Weald and Downland designated museum status.

The museum is continually developing and has over 45 buildings, representing the traditional homes and workplaces of village and countryside. Visitors can discover the working watermill rescued from Lurgashall, which produces stoneground wholemeal flour; the 16th century market hall from Titchfield, Hampshire; 19th century cottages from Ashtead in Surrey and, the jewel, a recreated medieval farmstead based on Bayleaf farmhouse, a Wealden hall house from Chiddingstone, Kent.

The Weald and Downland runs an ambitious programme in building conservation for professionals and interested individuals and has gained a national reputation for its standards in timber-building conservation especially. A complementary series of lifelong learning courses in rural skills is also offered each year, and there is a strong educational programme for school children.

The museum's priority is interpreting the buildings to a high standard and they are supported by period gardens, farm livestock, exhibitions on traditional building techniques, an important library, regular rural skills demonstrations and an annual programme of special events with countryside themes. The small staff and team of enthusiastic volunteers welcome some 140,000 visitors each year who enjoy the museum's magical mix of informality, education and recreation.

Cottages from Ashtead.

Bayleaf farmhouse.

A selection of the buildings, period gardens, farm livestock and activities at the museum. Albert Peacock from Fishbourne (below right) is pictured making thatching spars, a traditional woodland craft he has been practising for over 70 years.

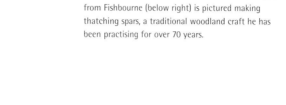

Buildings from the district include, left to right, the Walderton house, the Lurgashall watermill and the West Wittering school.

Heavy horses and a binder at work at the Northchapel steam fair

The 1999 Downs Steam Show, which was held at the Weald and Downland Open Air Museum.

A view from the Downs above Duncton Hill looking north to Petworth and Northchapel. Black Down can be seen in the far distance.

Mapsons farmhouse at Sidlesham, built by Thomas Hogben in 1796. The house is a splendid example of some of the Georgian farmhouses found on the coastal plain, reflecting the agricultural prosperity of the late 18th and early 19th century.

A timber-framed barn at Upwaltham. The district is still full of many interesting and beautifully constructed barns using convenient local materials. Brick, flint, stone, timber and clunch were commonly used and the barns sited where needed.

This small field barn can be seen near the South Downs Way on Bignor Hill.

Barn walling near Rotherbridge, Petworth, and at Ham, close to Sidlesham.

The Roman villa at Bignor was discovered in 1811 by a farmer, George Tupper, and the site is still owned by his descendants. Sited close to Stane Street, the villa would have been at the heart of a substantial agricultural estate and, by the 4th century, had been built to an exceptionally high standard encompassing a sophisticated bath suite and hypocaust providing under-floor heating. The spectacular mosaics, including the head of Medusa (below) and the head of Venus (above), are considered to be some of the best preserved in the country; whilst the north corridor is thought to have the longest mosaic on display.

Since the early 1990s, University College, London, under the supervision of its director, David Rudling, has carried out both student digs and educational courses on site. Among recent finds have been two infant burials, one, a female less than a year old, dating from the mid 2nd century. They are the only human remains to be found on site in almost 200 years of excavation.

The Roman palace at Fishbourne was discovered in 1960, when a workman cut into what proved to be the largest known Roman domestic building north of the Alps. It was one of the most important archaeological discoveries in Britain during the 20th century. Evidence suggests that the building may have been the palace of a local Celtic king, Togidubnus.

The most impressive development discovered on the site by the excavators was the construction of an enormous four-winged building around AD 75–80. This was recognised not only by its massive wall foundations but also by the remains of more than 20 mosaic floors. Many of these were black geometric patterns on a white background, a type popular in Italy at the time the building was constructed. However, some of these floors had been replaced in the 2nd and 3rd centuries and the replacements were polychrome and more representational. Of these, the most striking and most complete was the *Cupid on a Dolphin* mosaic. Here Cupid, holding a trident and sitting astride a dolphin, graces a central roundel, flanked by sea horses, sea panthers, wine vases and scallop shells. This whole design is enclosed by a border of spiral vine tendrils, on one of which perches a small black bird, perhaps the trademark of the mosaicist who designed it.

In the mid 1960s a protective cover was erected over the north wing remains and mosaic floors. A museum was built beside it to house the most important finds from the excavations. The museum display tells the story of the site using these objects along with plans, models and photographs. The whole site was opened to the public in 1968, and was visited by over 250,000 people in its first season and since then by almost four million people. More recently, attempts have been made to help visitors gain a better understanding of the site. One of the rooms of the north wing has been reconstructed and furnished to show what it would have been like around AD 100. In addition, the formal garden – while having been replanted as accurately as possible – did not give the visitor any idea of the wide range of plants grown by the Romans in their gardens. To solve this problem, a new Roman plant display area has been developed along with a museum of Roman gardens. The plant display has been put in a Roman setting, with raised beds, trellis fences, pergolas, arbours, water feature and an outdoor dining area or *triclinium*.

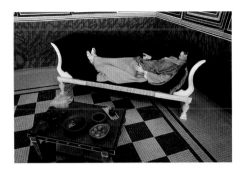

Vine arbours in the new Roman plant display area. Perhaps even more remarkable was the discovery, in the area enclosed by the four wings, of the original garden bedding trenches that had been dug out at the time of the construction of the palace. These have now been replanted using those plants most likely to have been use in the original. This means that the visitor today sees a garden very similar to that of 1,900 years ago.

The remains of a hypocaust or under-floor heating system in the north wing of the palace.

In 1995 the owners of the site, the Sussex Archaeological Society, decided to undertake further excavations at Fishbourne in an attempt to answer outstanding questions that had arisen since the 1960s excavations. One area of particular interest was the initial military activity on the site. Recently, a strong case had been put for the Roman invasion of AD 43 having taken place through Chichester Harbour, and it was hoped that further excavation might throw light on this. Five seasons of excavation were carried out in the field immediately to the east of the palace site. This revealed the foundations of a large masonry building, the ground plan of which strongly suggested a military headquarters building. This building appears to have been constructed around AD 50 and survived to around AD 200, despite the fact that c. AD 75–80 the palace was built a mere 50 metres to the west of it. The presence of such a building may suggest that Fishbourne had a far greater military significance than had previously been realised. These remains have now been reburied, but some of the finds may be seen in the museum.

Richard Williamson, the naturalist and retired warden to the Kingley Vale National Nature Reserve, is seen talking to a group on the top of the tumuli known as the 'Devil's Jumps' on Bow Hill, which looks down on Kingley Vale.

In 1974, aged 60, Alec Down was appointed Chichester's first full-time salaried archaeologist and effectively became the founding father of Chichester archaeology. His favourite part of West Sussex was the Chilgrove–Marden area. In the 1960s, he had excavated two villas in the Chilgrove Valley and later began investigating a third at Pitlands Farm, Up Marden, with the assistance of a well-drilled band of volunteers. His last major excavation, continuing beyond his retirement in 1986, was an Anglo-Saxon cemetery at Apple Down, Up Marden. He was author or co-author of nine substantial excavation reports, the last of which was in press when he died on Christmas Day 1995. This memorial to him is in Up Marden churchyard.

The Pitsham brickyard, near Cocking, has been in operation since 1869 and is a rare example of a small working country brickworks. It is owned by Lamb's Bricks and Arches, a company that specialises in producing clamp-burnt hand-made bricks for conservation projects.

Scenes on the River Rother. Stopham Bridge is regarded as one of the best examples of a medieval bridge. It marks the boundary of Chichester District, and a recently built new road bridge has brought much-needed relief from traffic. The bridge originates from 1309 and was rebuilt in 1423. The centre arch was raised in 1822 to accommodate barges using the Rother Navigation. The Rother Navigation was opened in 1794 and financed by the third Lord Egremont, principally for the improved efficiency of agriculture in the surrounding area.

Terwick Mill was still working until 1966 when it was the last of the Rother water mills to close down. The oldest parts date from at least the 17th century and it is now a private home. The mill straddles the River Rother on the footpath between Trotton and Dumpford. It is rather confusingly called Terwick as the only settlement which takes it name after the parish is at Terwick Common, and a few miles distant. The parish church is also some distance away, standing alone in the middle of a field, on the southern side of the A272.

The bridge at Stedham is thought to be 17th century in origin. It carries a warning by the County Council dated 1912 that steam engines should not loiter, and another notice forbidding the posting of bills on any part of the bridge. The western reaches of the Rother have a series of fine historic bridges at Durleighmarsh, Habin, Trotton, Chithurst and Iping.

The wharf at Newbridge on the Wey and Arun canal, near Wisborough Green. The warehouse is one of the few surviving canal buildings and was described by Cobbett as 'having large timber and coalyards and kilns for lime, and appearing to be a grand receiving and distributing place'.

Despite its proximity to the sea, Chichester District features several, mainly disused, canal routes. The narrowboat *Zachariah Keppel* has been specially converted to take trips on the Wey and Arun canal at Loxwood. Since its formation in 1970, the Canal Trust has been successful in restoring locks and bridges, as well as clearing sections of the canal. The Trust's ultimate objective is to reopen 'London's lost route to the sea', and make it possible again to travel from the Arun estuary at Littlehampton, through the heart of the Weald to the Thames. The canal was built to link the Rivers Arun and Wey and was completed in 1816, but went out of use in 1871.

At the time of taking this photograph, Elizabeth Girling still lived in the house she was born in nearly a hundred years ago. Her house is built on the site of the Portsmouth to Arundel canal at Runcton, which operated between 1823 and 1855. It was able to link Portsmouth via Chichester Harbour with the Arun Navigation and Wey and Arun canal but, as with the Chichester section, it was never a commercial success.

LEFT AND BELOW: Nostalgic reminders of the country railway. The Chichester to Midhurst railway line was opened in 1881 by the London, Brighton and South Coast Railway Co. It closed to passenger traffic in 1935, although a goods service was maintained until 1956, when the track between Lavant and Cocking was taken up. The line between Lavant and Chichester continued to be used during the late 1950s and early 1960s to carry sugar beet from local farms and, more recently, for moving gravel until it too was taken up in 1991.

Singleton, for a country station, was to experience many memorable occasions between its opening and 1914, through its association with Goodwood Racecourse and the regular visits of royalty to West Dean House. During the 1970s and 1980s the station house became a winery whilst the goods shed has for many years been used as an engineering workshop. The overgrown platforms and stairways now give a haunting and ghostly impression of the station's heyday.

BOTTOM RIGHT: Strangely, little visible evidence survives of the West Sussex Railway, or the Selsey Tram as it became affectionately called. Nostalgic photographs and personal memories of the line conjure up impressions of 'Thomas the Tank Engine'. Opened in 1897, the line's heyday was prior to the First World War when it took thousands of day-trippers and holidaymakers to the seaside. However, it was also important to the economy of the Manhood peninsula in other ways, including transporting the Selsey fishermen's crabs and lobsters and the Pullinger mousetraps, which were made in Selsey. After the First World War it faced increased competition from other means of private and public transport. Its service became more erratic and breakdowns were frequent, resulting eventually in its closure in 1935. Part of the old track bed forms a public footpath known as the Selsey Tram Way.

The entrance to Cocking tunnel, which measures 675 metres in length. The tunnels on the line, driven through the chalk, were an incredible engineering achievement for their time. The navvies who built them were described as a wild, hard-drinking lot. One was charged with 'smashing a quart pot against a policeman's head'. In a broadcast from Germany during the Second World War, the traitor William Joyce ('Lord Haw-Haw') mentioned that the tunnels at Cocking and Singleton were being used to store ammunition. This possibly led to a German bombing raid taking place nearby.

The interior of the former booking hall of Petworth station. The station house is the second to have been built on the site and dates from the early 1890s. It is said that Lord Leconfield was instrumental in ensuring that the station was built out of sight and sound of Petworth House. Like Singleton, it received a number of royal and important passengers who were visiting Petworth House. The line closed in 1966 and the present owners, Mike and Mary-Louise Rapley, have converted the station and two former Pullman carriages into unusual and award-winning bed and breakfast accommodation.

Fetes of all descriptions, together with horticultural shows and fund-raising events for churches, village halls, schools and other needy projects take place each weekend throughout the summer months. The following scenes were taken at North Mundham, Lavant, South Harting, Lodsworth, Chidham and Runcton.

132

The countryside is particularly rich in its use of different local building materials, ranging from the sea-rounded cobblestones and 'Mixon' stone of the coastal plain, the flint and chalk clunch to be found in the Downland villages and the buff, grey or green coloured stone of the Lower Greensand found in the buildings around Petworth and Midhurst. It is, however, timber that was most commonly used in all traditional building, until 'the great rebuilding'

132

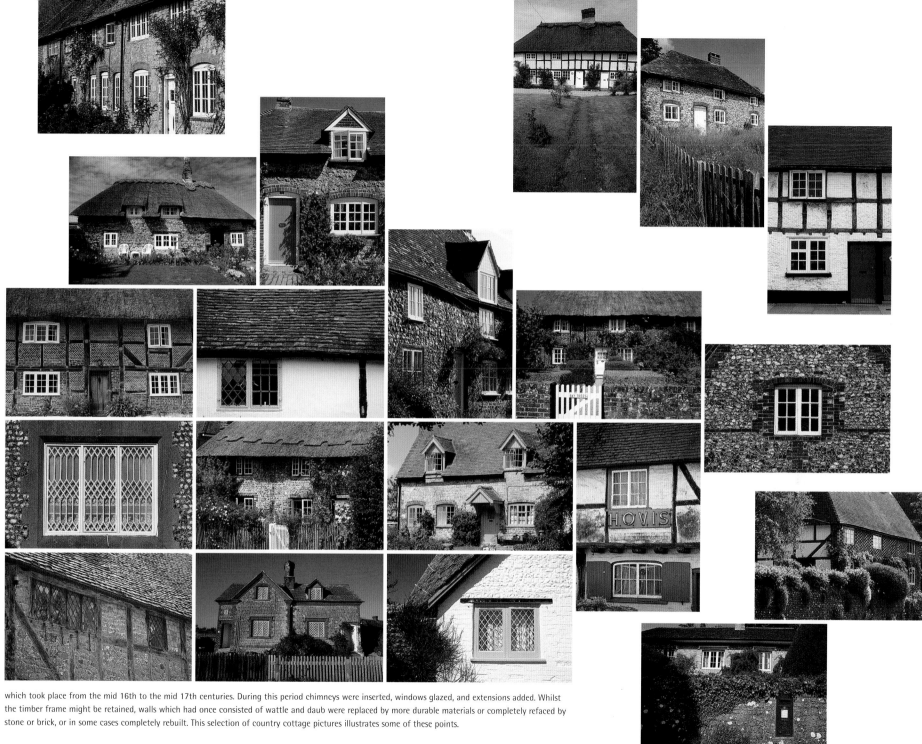

which took place from the mid 16th to the mid 17th centuries. During this period chimneys were inserted, windows glazed, and extensions added. Whilst the timber frame might be retained, walls which had once consisted of wattle and daub were replaced by more durable materials or completely refaced by stone or brick, or in some cases completely rebuilt. This selection of country cottage pictures illustrates some of these points.

Brinkwells, near Fittleworth was the home of Sir
Edward Elgar between 1917 and 1921 and is where he
wrote the *Cello Concerto*. He was very fond of his
primitive cottage, which he described as 'too lovely for
words'. When visiting in 1967, Bernard Price wrote: 'An
old cart track springs away from the deep road with its
high banks and tall trees. The track is rutted and falls
away steeply, going on to nowhere, and there tucked
away in the bluebell woods is Brinkwells'.

Fittleworth Common consists
of open woodland and is
typical of a piece of Sussex
Greensand heathland.

At the start of the 20th century, Edward VII was concerned at the prevalence of pulmonary tuberculosis. As a result the King Edward VII sanatorium built just to the north of Midhurst, was conceived for the care of good persons of limited means. Sir Ernest Cassel was the benefactor who contributed £200,000. Edward VII laid the foundation stone in 1903 and declared the sanatorium open in 1906. During the First World War, in addition to civilian patients, it accommodated service personnel suffering from tuberculosis. During the Second World War, the Emergency Medical Services became responsible for 40 beds of which 30 were used for the RAF. In addition to the tuberculosis patients, casualties from the Services requiring chest surgery were admitted.

When the National Health Service came into being in 1948, the sanatorium remained private, but the Regional Hospital Board funded some of the beds, and allowed the admission of some NHS patients. With the advent of antibiotics and a cure for pulmonary tuberculosis, the waiting lists vanished. In 1964, the sanatorium was given the title of 'hospital'. Patients with other chest conditions were admitted and more surgery was carried out. Gradually the hospital has diversified to cope with any condition. The Macmillan Care Service for cancer relief has operated from the hospital since 1976. The hospital also owns the Sherburne hospital in Broyle Road, Chichester, opened in 1992.

OPPOSITE: A misty view from Bury Hill. The author of *The Forsyte Saga*, John Galsworthy, lived the latter years of his life at Bury House. He died in 1933 and his ashes were scattered on Bury Hill.

A selection of evocative Downland landscapes.

Racing at Goodwood was begun by the third Duke of Richmond in 1801. The meeting soon became established as an important occasion in the social calendar at the end of July. The fifth Duke erected a new grandstand in 1830 and improvements were carried out to the course under the direction of Lord George Bentinck. The famous Stewards' Cup race was introduced in 1840.

King Edward VII's sentiment that racing at Goodwood is 'a garden party with racing tacked on' has been echoed down the years by racegoers and this unique atmosphere makes Goodwood the place to be and be seen. Due to Edward VII's influence panama hats gradually replaced the more formal racing attire of top hat and tails.

Since the building of the March Stand in 1980, designed by Sir Philip Dowson, which replaced the Edwardian grandstand, the racecourse has undergone a phased programme of redevelopment, including the introduction of evening and Sunday racing. Racing now takes place on 20 days each year.

A programme of new and improved facilities for racegoers is planned, including the redevelopment of the parade ring, weighing-in building, and the winner's enclosure. The completion of the work in 2002 will coincide with the 200th anniversary of racing at Goodwood under Jockey Club Rules.

Motor racing first came to Goodwood in 1936 when the Earl of March held a private hill climb through the park for the Lancia Car Club. Five years earlier Freddie March had won the Brooklands Doubles 12. In 1948, as the ninth Duke of Richmond, he opened the Goodwood circuit. The circuit was built on the Westhampnett airfield, now Goodwood aerodrome, a satellite airfield to RAF Tangmere during the Second World War, but racing finished in the 1960s. These early events inspired his grandson Charles March to revive motor sport in the park and resulted in the inaugural Goodwood Festival of Speed in 1993 and the Motor Circuit Revival meeting in 1998.

Both events have been phenomenal successes and attract stars and cars from every corner of motor racing's hall of fame. Names such as Stirling Moss, John Surtees, Jack Brabham, Jackie Stewart, Phil Hill, Barry Sheene and Damon Hill, return to relive the glory days of British racing green. At the Revival meeting, spectators wearing period dress of the post-war era, as well as displays by Spitfires and Messerschmitts, help to make Goodwood a time capsule for three days of spectacular entertainment.

These pictures give a mosaic of the inaugural Goodwood Motor Circuit Revival meeting in September 1998, which was also the 50th anniversary of the opening of this historic circuit. Included (below) is a picture of the Duke and Duchess of Richmond and Gordon together with the Earl and Countess of March and their son Lord Settrington. The scene opposite is at the start of the very first race since closure.

Cricket at Goodwood. The Hampshire village of Hambledon is more popularly looked upon as being the birthplace of English cricket. However, the Goodwood Estate can claim to have stronger links with the game's roots. The first reference to cricket being played in Sussex is in 1622 at Boxgrove priory. The second Duke of Richmond who jointly drew up the first recorded laws of the game in 1727 and local men such as the Lillywhite family played an influential part in the game's development over the next two centuries. This scene shows the match outside Goodwood House prior to the Motor Circuit Revival meeting in 1998.

The Festival of Speed in Goodwood Park. A Ferrari passes the Audi display stand in front of the house (above).

Goodwood House has been the home of the Dukes of Richmond for 300 years. The original house was built as a hunting lodge by the ninth Earl of Northumberland in the early 17th century. The Long Hall still survives as part of the present house, which was primarily built at the beginning of the 19th century by James Wyatt for the third Duke. The house and a number of buildings on the estate, including the magnificent stable block by Sir William Chambers, contain some of the finest examples of 'knapped' flintwork to be found.

The Yellow Drawing Room was part of the great Regency extensions to the house for the third Duke by James Wyatt. In the 1820s it was hung with glowing yellow/amber silk, for the fifth Duke, and the Axminster carpet was woven especially. By the 1970s the silk had deteriorated beyond repair. In order to recreate the original scheme, 350 metres of silk were newly woven in England. The room is adorned with French 18th century furniture.

The Egyptian Dining Room, created by the third Duke between 1802 and 1806 when Napoleon's campaign on the Nile had caused great public interest in Egypt. The scheme survived nearly 100 years before being taken down in 1903. In 1996 it was recreated by the Earl of March. The original scagliola walls were exposed and the details keep as close as possible to the original.

During the last half of the 17th and first half of the 18th century, Charlton was the home of the country's premier foxhunt. The ill-fated Duke of Monmouth hunted at Charlton and it is said that he wanted to establish his court there should he become king. Another of Charles II's sons, the first Duke of Richmond, was also a keen huntsman. He purchased Goodwood, a small hunting box near Charlton. Fox Hall, a hunting lodge, was built in the village by the second Duke in about 1730. The architect was either Lord Burlington or Roger Morris. It has been restored by the Landmark Trust and is let as holiday accommodation.

Rod Fabricius, Goodwood's clerk of the course, with the grounds manager and assistant clerk of the course, Seamus Buckley, carrying out an early morning race-day 'going' inspection.

Carné's Seat in Goodwood Park enjoys spectacular views towards Chichester and the coast. Designed by Roger Morris in 1743 for the second Duke, it contained a banqueting room on the first floor. It is named after Philippe de Carné, a former retainer of Louise de Keroualle, who had lived on the site. A signal would be made from the building to Itchenor when the third Duke wanted his yacht prepared for sailing.

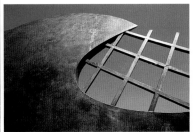

Founded and privately endowed by Wilfred and Jeannette Cass in 1994, Sculpture at Goodwood is a charitable foundation dedicated to commissioning, promoting and selling contemporary British sculpture. With over 100 sculptures realised in its first five years, Sculpture at Goodwood is helping British sculpture gain a higher profile nationally and internationally. In forming partnerships with artists, Goodwood also works with other organisations to assist projects outside its own boundaries. As well as working in partnership with the London Contemporary Art Fair on the Sculpture at Goodwood ART2000 commission prize, Goodwood has jointly initiated the Fourth Plinth Project with the RSA. For the year 2000, the foundation has enabled two new sculptures for the Millennium Dome, North Meadow Arts Project and has commissioned and loaned 12 pieces for the 'Bronze' exhibition at Holland Park to open in April 2000. Ten hectares of woodland walks and glades provide an idyllic venue for the changing displays of outdoor sculpture.

Included in this mosaic of photographs are works by Steven Gregory, Laura Ford, Peter Randall Page, Keir Smith, Zadok Ben David, Stephen Cox, Mark Firth, Peter Burke, Allen Jones and Nigel Ellis.

West Dean House is one of the finest flint mansions in the country and stands on ground that has been occupied since medieval times. In 1891 the house and its estate were bought by Mr Willie James. His wife, Evelyn, became one of Edwardian society's best known hostesses. At this time, Edward, Prince of Wales, later King Edward VII, was a frequent visitor to West Dean. Other royal visitors included Queen Alexandra, the future King George V and Queen Mary, and King Alfonso XIII of Spain.

Mr Willie James died in 1912 and his estate was held in trust until his son, Edward, (1907–1984) came of age. Edward was a poet and a major patron of the arts, particularly of the artists Salvador Dali and Rene Magritte. In consequence he amassed one of the finest and most important collections of surrealist art in the world. After the Second World War he spent much time abroad, living principally in Mexico. In 1964 he established the Edward James Foundation as a charitable educational trust. The house became a college where traditional arts and crafts and the conservation and restoration of antiques are taught to a professional level. The college runs building conservation masterclass courses in a recently restored Victorian dairy building nearby, using a unique artificial ruin built from a variety of natural materials.

The house is surrounded by 14 hectares of gardens. There are water and wild gardens, through which the River Lavant flows, and a 300-foot long pergola designed by Harold Peto. The Edwardian walled kitchen garden, with its greenhouses and frames, has been completely restored in recent years, faithful to its turn of the century origins. It provides for visitors the atmosphere and ambience of the turn of the century when the walled gardens were at their zenith. In 1996, the Prince of Wales opened the gardens' visitor centre, a beautifully crafted building built using both estate-grown timber and other local materials. It was the first working building in the country to have been constructed in association with the Prince of Wales's Institute of Architecture.

Each year, West Dean celebrates a cornucopia of produce with a chilli fiesta, tomato show, and apple day, according to season.

Head gardeners at West Dean – Jim Buckland and his wife Sarah Wain – in one of the newly restored kitchen garden greenhouses.

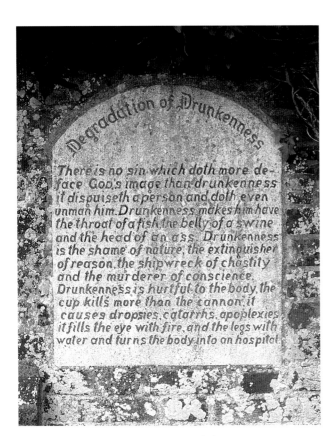

This warning to all pub goers can be found at Kirdford.

Singleton and East Dean Women's Institute was the first one to be formed in England. The inaugural meeting took place on 9th November 1915 in the Fox Inn, Charlton. The WI seen here at the Fox continues to flourish.

The following are a selection of the many country and village pubs and inns to be found in the district.

The Lickfold Inn. Formerly called the Three Horse Shoes, this popular name for an inn was a sign that a farrier was at hand to re-shoe a traveller's horse.

The White Horse at Sutton has been operating as the village inn for at least 250 years.

The Gribble Inn at Oving. Named after its former owner, it was only converted into a pub 20 years ago. It has its own brewery, which can produce up to 4,320 pints per week.

The Bader Arms, at Tangmere. Named after the famous Battle of Britain fighter pilot, who had been Squadron Leader of the Tangmere Wing of the three Spitfire squadrons.

The Duke of Cumberland at Henley. The main London road once passed through the hamlet and the inn was used as a staging post for changing horses. It is possible that the inn's name originates from the second half of the 18th century after the Duke of Cumberland who had routed the Scots at the Battle of Culloden in 1746.

The Noah's Ark at Lurgashall. The name is thought to have originated from about 1700 because, at that time, the entrance could only be accessed across a pond thus giving the effect of the animals having to cross into Noah's ark. Lurgashall is a quintessential English village and the inn, which hosts an annual summer play, is in a delightful spot overlooking the village green.

The White Horse Inn at Chilgrove. The white cat on the inn sign is said to deter birds nesting in the wisteria growing along the inn's façade. It came about because the artist commissioned to paint a new sign preferred to paint cats to horses!

The Old House at Chidham. The inn dates from the 17th century and has been a focal point for the inhabitants of this tiny peninsula overlooking the harbour.

The Cricketers at Duncton. The village has some interesting 19th century Sussex cricketing associations. A Duncton farmer, Jem Broadbridge, together with William Lillywhite, were pioneers of the round arm bowling action. Broadbridge's nephew, Jem Dean, another notable Sussex player, is portrayed on the inn's sign.

The Royal Oak at Hooksway. Its landlord from 1907 to 1971 was Alf Ainger, during which time he and the pub became part of local folklore. His many reminiscences included a visit from King Edward VII whilst out shooting on the West Dean estate. Alf is probably best known for the reply he gave to the Midhurst licensing magistrate when he was asked what toilet facilities were available: 'I got nine acres, sir'.

Ballard's, a small independent brewery, near Rogate, has become well known for its local beers which include brand names like Midhurst Mild, Trotton Bitter, Wassail, and the 1999 annual brew, Trout Tickler. The brewery is run by Carola Brown. It began life in a cowshed on her family farm in 1980, before moving to the Ballard's pub, the Elsted Inn at Elsted Marsh. Head brewer, Francis Weston, in the picture, produces some 1,500 gallons of beer each week from the brewery's current premises at Nyewood.

The village shop, the local pub, school and church, are bastions of our rural communities. They have all had to cope with the economic and social changes that have affected village life during the second half of the 20th century. The village pub now has to compete with the new urban trend of 'theme' pubs, and has had to diversify, serving less beer but providing meals, and bed and breakfast. The shop has been particularly affected as the rural population has become increasingly mobile and lured to do their shopping at supermarkets. Many shops have been forced to close or have been converted into private homes. Others offer bed and breakfast or serve afternoon teas, and many are off-licences and video outlets.

The village shop performs a vital role, not only as a store, but also as a post office, newsagent, and meeting point where the latest village news can be exchanged. In an age when shopping can be done from a computer, they offer a personal service. Many villages have fought to save their shops, and Graffham is an example where the property is actually owned by the community.

Since taking these photographs, the shop at Tillington closed in October 1999.

OPPOSITE: Merston church stall – a voluntary produce stall started in 1993 and operated once a week throughout the summer to raise funds for St Giles' church. Founded by Bob and Audrey Fogden and helped by Jean Palmer and Joan Johns, all senior citizens, the produce is entirely home grown and in the six years of running the stall, over £10,000 has been raised to help with the planned church re-roofing.

Village cricket. A cricket match is played at Ebernoe each year on St James'
Day (25th July) against local village rivals Lurgashall, to celebrate the Horn
Fair. Tradition has it that the highest-scoring batsman on the winning team is
presented with the horns of a sheep that has been roasted whilst the match
has been in progress.

The epitome of an English summer's scene at
Wisborough Green.

A summer's afternoon at Tillington.

Ladies cricket at Bury. Ladies cricket has been played in Sussex since at least 1747 when 'the Maids of Charlton and Singleton played those of West Dean and Chilgrove' at the Artillery Ground in London. It was reported that the match had to be suspended due to crowd trouble!

The churchyard at Westhampnett, contains the gravestone to James Lillywhite who captained England in the first two Test matches played in Australia in 1876–77. In an age when sport is dominated by money and sponsorship deals, an interesting story connects Lillywhite and Charles Stride, the founder of Stride and Son. Stride and another local family, the Hogbens, helped to finance the tour. On his return Lillywhite is said to have given back to Stride a sum exceeding £4,000 with the remark 'and that is what there is left over'!

The South Downs Way was the first long-distance bridleway in the country to be designated by the former Countryside Commission (now the Countryside Agency) in 1972. It is a popular recreational resource for walkers, cyclists and horse-riders, and now stretches 100 miles (160 kilometres) from Eastbourne to Winchester. The path in Sussex is maintained by the Sussex Downs Conservation Board, on behalf of the highway authority, and under the guidance of the South Downs Way Officer. These photographs show the section between Bignor Hill and the new footpath bridge over the River Arun near Houghton.

OPPOSITE: The partial eclipse of the sun being watched from the ramparts of the Trundle on 11th August 1999. This was the final eclipse of the old millennium.

The Chichester International March, was renewed in August 1998 with 2,000 participants, and is seen here passing Goodwood House. The march was founded by the Royal Military Police in 1977 and attracted many thousands of participants from home and abroad, until Government cutbacks in 1993 forced the RMP to terminate its support.

In 1996 Chichester twinned with Ravenna in Italy and on a visit to the ceramic museum at Faensa, the then Mayor of Chichester (Councillor Mrs Clare Apel) was approached by two Italians who were wearing medals from every RMP March that had taken place. They asked her when the march was going to be resumed. Upon her return, she formed a committee with her deputy and successor as mayor, Councillor Ray Brown. They co-opted the Police, the Fire Brigade, the Royal Artillery and the Fellowship Societies (notably the Rotary and Lions) and together they presided over the staging of the renewed march. The International March is now firmly on Chichester's calendar once more and a special millennium march is planned.

Cyclists on the South Downs Way near Bignor Hill.

Tangmere Military Aviation Museum was founded by a few dedicated volunteers and opened in 1982. The museum's collections relate to military flying from its earliest days, with a particular emphasis on the history of RAF Tangmere and the air war over southern England from 1939 to 1945. The museum is housed in buildings, which date from the 1930s and were once used as radio repair workshops. A new hangar was built in 1992 and houses the actual Meteor and Hunter jet aircraft which broke the world air speed record in 1946 and 1953 respectively, flying from Tangmere. There is a large collection of photographs, paintings, documents, uniforms and medals which illustrate the story of this famous fighter airfield from its establishment in 1917 to its closure in 1970.

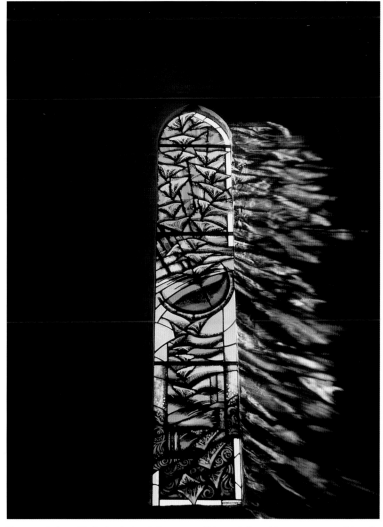

The west window of St Andrew's church, Tangmere, which was dedicated in 1999 as a memorial to all those who served at RAF Tangmere. RAF Tangmere played a major part in the Battle of Britain during the summer and autumn of 1940. Despite the station suffering severe damage in one raid by German dive-bombers, the Tangmere squadrons were instrumental in ensuring that the Luftwaffe failed in their efforts to overcome the RAF during this critical stage of the Second World War. The station also played a crucial role in the build up to the D-Day landings. Many famous pilots were stationed at Tangmere, including the legendary Douglas Bader who was Squadron Leader of the Tangmere wing of three Spitfire squadrons. He was at Tangmere from April 1941 until he was shot down over France in August that year. Tangmere was the advanced base for the Special Duties Squadron, which parachuted agents behind enemy lines. The gravestones in St Andrew's churchyard commemorate both Allied and German pilots who lost their lives during the war.

The name Thorney Island is derived from its Saxon name the 'thorn tree island'. It was an important RAF base from 1938 to 1976 and, like St Andrew's church, Tangmere, gravestones in St Nicholas' churchyard commemorate both Allied and German pilots who lost their lives during the Second World War. Bernard Price mentions that the novelist Ernest Hemingway was briefly stationed at Thorney Island whilst serving as a war correspondent. Between 1979 and 1981, the station became a re-settlement base for Vietnamese refugees and currently it serves as a base for the Royal Artillery.

CHICHESTER HARBOUR
AND
THE SEA

Managed by Chichester Harbour Conservancy, Chichester Harbour extends to some 11 square miles of inter-tidal waters and 17 miles of navigable channels. Between the 17th and 19th centuries it was a busy commercial harbour, exporting wool, wheat and malt. For nearly a hundred years the Chichester canal linked the harbour to the extensive waterway transport system of this country. Today the harbour has virtually no commercial traffic, but provides ideal water space for recreational sailing, angling, and a base for a small but active fleet of professional fishermen. Nearly 12,000 vessels are on record at the harbour office paying annual harbour dues. There are six marinas, sixteen sailing clubs and associations, four sailing schools and activity centres, and fifteen boatyards supporting the substantial water-based recreation within Chichester Harbour and the Solent area. Chichester Harbour Water Tours based at West Itchenor accommodate visitors wishing to tour the harbour by boat and view its wildlife.

The villages and hamlets of the Manhood Peninsula and Chichester Harbour are shrouded in myth and legend going back to Roman times. It is now considered a possibility that the harbour was a bridgehead for the Roman invasion of Britain. Many place names are Saxon in origin such as those ending with the suffix *ham*, referring to a homestead, hence the names Sidel's ham and Bosa's ham; or Itchenor, which is a derivation of Iccanore or 'Icca's landing'. The village of Bosham is seen here opposite at high tide.

Bosham quay and the Raptackle.

Holy Trinity church at Bosham may have been built on the site of a small monastery that is said to have existed prior to the coming of St Wilfrid. Bosham was an important Saxon settlement, and the church tower dates from this time. It is probable that the powerful nobleman, Godwin, Earl of Essex, had a residence at Bosham. The Bayeux Tapestry shows Godwin's son, Harold, praying at Bosham church in 1064 prior to his ill-fated journey across the Channel. He was shipwrecked off the coast of Normandy and fell into the hands of Duke William. The Normans claimed that, before returning to England, Harold took an oath renouncing his claim to the English throne. Harold subsequently became king on the death of Edward the Confessor in 1066 and this led to the Norman invasion that changed the course of English history. Bosham has, over the centuries, been well known for shipbuilding and as a fishing port, but today it is best known as a recreational sailing centre.

Bosham from across Bosham channel.

Unsuspecting motorists at Bosham often return to find their cars have been caught by an incoming tide. Although modern historians have dismissed the story, legend has it that it was at Bosham that King Canute (who reigned 1016 to 1035) sat in his chair and attempted to command the tide to turn back. The discovery of a child's tomb in the church during the Victorian period led to speculation that it might have been that of Canute's daughter.

Sunset over Chichester Harbour at Cobnor Point on the tip of the Chidham peninsula. Chidham is also known for a small piece of agricultural history. At the end of the 18th century a variety of wheat, known as Chidham wheat, was discovered and became famous for its prolific yield of grain. A crop is still grown at the Weald and Downland Open Air Museum.

A few stones are all that remain of the foundations to the tidal salt mill which stood at the entrance to the millpond in Fishbourne Creek, captured here on a misty morning. A causeway, which was also part of the mill pond embankment, leads out to it. The former millpond has become a haven for bird life and another footpath leads through the reed beds that have now grown in the silt at the head of the pond. Fishbourne had, at one time during the 19th century, three mills and a windmill. Salt making was once an important industry in the harbour and at Apuldram, just to the south, salterns were used in the making of the medicinal Epsom and Glauber salts.

Recreational sailing is now the main activity at Dell Quay. Despite being one and a half miles from the city the wharf at Dell Quay was, from medieval times, Chichester's nearest accessible port and a key factor in its prosperity. Coal, corn, timber and wool were the main goods imported and exported through Dell Quay.

Sailing centres include Bosham, West Itchenor, Dell Quay and Emsworth. Marinas are at Birdham Pool, Chichester Yacht Basin, Hayling Island, Emsworth and Thorney Island. Chichester Yacht Basin, adjacent to Birdham Pool, is shown here on a crowded day.

Birdham Pool was one of the first purpose-built yachting marinas in the country. It was developed during the late 1930s following the closure of the 18th century mill and its tidal mill pool.

Houseboats and water lilies are now resident on the last stretch of the canal at the Chichester Yacht Basin where the canal emerges into the harbour.

Some interesting associations between Itchenor and Goodwood can be drawn from references by J. Reger in his book about Chichester Harbour. There is an unsubstantiated story that Charles II's yacht *The Fubs* was commanded by an Itchenor man, Captain Darley. Charles affectionately nicknamed his mistress, Louise de Keroualle, 'my dearest, dearest Fubs', on account of her plumpness, and the yacht was named after her. She was mother to the first Duke of Richmond, whose grandson, the third Duke, built Itchenor House as a yachting lodge during the 1780s, complete with adjoining racing stables and a terrace of cottages in the main street running down to the harbour.

Sir Jeremy Thomas outside Waterstones bookshop in Chichester following the launch of his successful first novel *The Rhythm of the Tide*, about Chichester Harbour, which was published in 1999. Sir Jeremy recalls his first sighting of the harbour in 1937 aged six, coming into the entrance from Selsey in his uncle's boat and landing at East Head. He started sailing himself at Itchenor in 1946 and has been a member of the Chichester Harbour Conservancy Advisory Committee since 1989 and its chairman between 1993 and 1997. He is also a trustee of Cobnor Activities Centre Trust and currently its chairman. The centre has just opened a new facilities building and is used by nearly 4,000 young people each year participating in a number of water- and land-based activities.

Harbour walk and cream tea. Judi Darley, whose family has long associations with the harbour, is the Education and Interpretation Warden for the Harbour Conservancy. She is photographed leading a harbour walk around the sand dunes of East Head, which will be followed by a cream tea at the Beach House Restaurant, West Wittering.

OPPOSITE: Boats at Snow Hill Creek near West Wittering belonging to members of West Wittering Sailing Club. The place is probably named after a local family called Snow, rather than a reference to wintry weather conditions. There were once oyster beds in the creek and old maps show the creek extending inland almost as far as West Wittering church. This may explain the existence of coastguard cottages nearby.

OPPOSITE: Winter emptiness at East Head. Despite the often crowded beaches in summer, East Head can equally be enjoyed in winter without another soul in sight. The quickly changing tides and light give a totally different atmosphere of space and peace.

Summer boating at East Head. East Head is a sand dune spit at the eastern entrance to Chichester Harbour. It is owned by the National Trust and is a popular spot for a whole range of visitors from yachtsmen, picnickers and sunbathers to ecologists, ornithologists and walkers. The dunes are particularly sensitive to human damage, as well as wind and storm damage and require constant maintenance to help conserve them. With the salt marsh behind, they form one of the country's rarest natural habitats.

The unspoilt sandy beach by the entrance to Chichester Harbour at West Wittering has been popular with bathers since the 1920s, and more recently with windsurfers. In 1998 it was classed as the best beach in the United Kingdom, regularly receiving clean beach and water quality awards. In 1954, the Church Commissioners put up the beach and surrounding land for sale. In order to rescue it from holiday camp and caravan park development, local residents formed the West Wittering Protection Society, now West Wittering Estate plc, which still owns and manages it. This is a crowded scene on a hot August afternoon.

The Schneider Trophy, an international trophy open to seaplanes, was contested off West Wittering in 1931 and won outright by Great Britain. The contest was watched by Sir Henry Royce, the famous engineer who had designed the winning Merlin Aero engine. He lived in the village, and a wall plaque marks his drawing office there.

Windsurfers at Bracklesham Bay.

Selsey is well favoured with its clear skies and atmosphere. The astronomer Dr Patrick Moore – Selsey's most famous resident – is shown here in his garden observatory with one of his many telescopes. Dr Moore is patron of an exciting project to create the South Downs Planetarium in Chichester during the new millennium.

East Beach at Selsey, looking towards the lifeboat station built in 1960. A small museum in the station tells the story of the Selsey lifeboat. The station replaced an earlier one, built in 1927, the distance from the shore having moved in the intervening period by nearly half a mile as a result of coastal erosion. The current Selsey lifeboat is the *City of London*, a Tyne class lifeboat. The boat, on average, answers about 25 distress calls each year. As a fishing village, Selsey has always been famous for its shellfish, particularly crabs and lobsters. During the Second World War, the floating Mulberry harbours used for the D-Day landings were constructed here. In more recent times it became well known for its caravan parks and as a holiday resort.

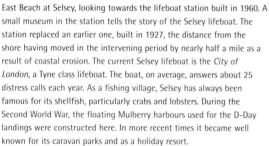

Selsey fisherman 'Honest' Bill Arnell by his fish shop at East Beach. Bill started fishing at the age of 14 during the late 1920s, when he recalls that the Selsey fishing fleet consisted of about 70 boats and 100 fishermen. In those days, they were all rowing and sailing boats and relied on the stars and a compass for navigation. The crabs, lobsters and prawns would be sent to Billingsgate market in London and also to Brighton and, until its closure in 1935, the Selsey Tram would transport the catch as far as Chichester. Bill recalls the names of some of the six Selsey Tram engines, such as the *Ringing Rock*, *Selsey* and *Wembley*. Today, there are only about half the numbers of fishermen and the shellfish caught are sold to the French and Spanish markets.

Selsey Bill is the most southerly point on the Sussex coast. Selsey was, in effect, an island until the early 19th century, and this exposed peninsula has been gradually eroding away for centuries. At the new millennium, the coastline is even more under threat, particularly the West Beach, and decisions are pending on whether to invest in further sea defences.

OPPOSITE: Pagham Harbour is one of the few undeveloped areas of the coast in West Sussex. The open landscape still retains a sense of wilderness and is very popular with ornithologists. The harbour was reclaimed for agriculture in the late 19th century, but was flooded again by a storm in the early 20th century. The harbour and the surrounding pasture are of international importance for wintering wildfowl and waders. The County Council has managed the area since 1964 as a local nature reserve. Extending to some 600 hectares, the reserve encompasses a mosaic of habitats including large areas of salt marsh and mudflats intermingled with shingle beaches, reed beds and wet grasslands.

TOWARDS
THE
NEW MILLENNIUM

As January 2000 gradually grew nearer, many individuals, groups, committees and villages began to consider ideas or projects to commemorate the new millennium. This section of the book shows just a few of these projects, sometimes in the initial planning stages, to mark this momentous occasion, and some of the celebrations that followed shortly after.

OPPOSITE: Towards the end of the old millennium. A winter sunset over Pagham Harbour looking west to Church Norton and St Wilfrid's chapel.

The chapel is all that remains of Selsey's former parish church, which was removed from Church Norton to its present-day site in Selsey in 1866, leaving only the chancel. It dates from the 13th century, and it has been speculated that the original church may have been built on or near the site of St Wilfrid's cathedral church. Archaeological excavations carried out on the earthworks surrounding the churchyard revealed the site as having a square Norman tower. There were 25 Bishops of Selsey between 681 and 1075, before the bishopric was transferred to Chichester almost a thousand years ago.

The new millennium stained glass window recently installed at All Hallows church, Tillington, near Petworth. The design is based on the theme of baptism and depicts various religious symbols including a fish, a lamb, day and night, and God as the all-seeing eye. The artist, Reg Lloyd RI, was commissioned to design the window by resident and former parochial church council member, George Warren. George organised the appeal for the necessary finance for the window and succeeded in raising well over £6,500 from local people. This money has been used not only to cover the costs of the new window, but also for moving the previous window to a new site within the church and for providing an information plaque.

Tillington church is best known because of its tower with the distinctive Scots crown of flying buttresses. The dramatic effect of this design is shown at its best in Turner's landscapes of Petworth Park.

A small committee from Milland outside the Milland Memorial Hall, about to discuss further plans for the proposed extension and refurbishment of the building. Due to considerable fund-raising efforts by villagers, a large amount of money has been raised over three years to help finance this millennium-based project. It is hoped that with help from lottery funding the new works will be completed towards the end of 2000 giving much-needed facilities and a focal point to further the village social and community spirit.

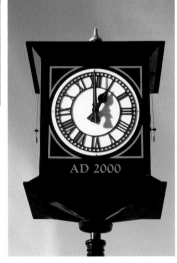

The new millennium clock sited in East Wittering shopping centre. The clock has been installed as a result of the villagers desire to mark the millennium in some form. Money has been raised for the project by the Witterings Chamber of Commerce and in particular by resident Lesley Moore. Not only has enough finance been collected for the clock itself in just over six months, but further monies are also available to install security cameras within the shopping centre. It is also hoped to provide a landscaped area around the clock giving a focal point for the area.

A member of the Chichester District Museum staff preparing the museum's millennium exhibition, *Chichester – A Century of Change*. The museum works with people throughout the area to help them uncover their own local histories. At the museum, visitors can trace the story of Chichester and artefacts from everyday life throughout the ages. The displays also show Chichester's changing role as a market centre. As well as study collections and local memories there are many activities and handling sessions – a chance to touch the past. The museum offers a growing programme of children's events, study groups and changing exhibitions.

Number 29 Little London was converted to form a home for Chichester's museum in 1963 The building was formerly a corn store. In the early 1900s it was bought by Sadler and Co., agricultural merchants. At this time trades linked with local agriculture were still vital to the prosperity of the Chichester area. By the 1960s this had changed and several buildings in Little London fell into disuse. The architect Stanley Roth was instrumental in preserving the street as it is today. Several original features remain including a large crane on the side of the building once used for hoisting sacks. A story which claims that the street was named Little London by Queen Elizabeth I on her visit to the city must be regarded as false because there is reference to the name a century earlier.

Kim Leslie in the Chichester West Sussex County Record Office with some completed millennium maps. Right across the county, West Sussex people are mapping where they live at the turn of the millennium. This vast and ambitious project, involving a network of hundreds of volunteers, is being directed by Kim who masterminds heritage projects for West Sussex County Council.

The parish maps they are making are pictorial and highly decorative – most are painted, but some are embroidered. They focus on key local features such as significant buildings, topographical scenes and wildlife, with snippets of information about life today, local lore and customs. They are the ingredients that give a place its own very special identity; something that is under threat today. To Kim, this is one of the main reasons why this project is so important. As he says, these maps heighten awareness about a sense of place and are all about capturing the spirit and feel of the county.

Sussex born and bred, Kim readily admits his interest in his native county is a passion. For many years now he has been promoting local studies in West Sussex through teaching, lecturing and writing, as well as advising individuals and organisations on compiling their own parish histories.

Marking the millennium again, Kim has just completed co-editing *An Historical Atlas of Sussex* which surveys the history of the county from geological and prehistoric times to the year 2000. He has also recently embarked on his next major project, Chichester Harbour Conservancy's millennium archive project, gathering memories and information about the harbour in the 20th century before it is all lost and forgotten.

A Christmas and millennium exhibition organised by the Friends of Pagham Harbour of photographs, watercolours and drawings created by both professional and amateur artists on display at the Pagham Harbour Visitors Centre, Sidlesham. The exhibition relates to the harbour and its wildlife and all items have been for sale with a proportion being donated to the Friends.

Arnold Hooton, a retired graphic designer, puts the finishing touches to the North Mundham parish millennium map. Inspired by Kim Leslie's enthusiasm for the millennium maps, a small committee from the parish was formed with the intention of producing, firstly a map and later a book, covering the parish history and its appearance at the start of the 21st century. Arnold carried out all the map artwork and it is a great credit to his artistic skills. The parish, covering the villages of North and South Mundham and Runcton, supported the project by buying over 400 copies of the map within a few weeks of its official launch. Further copies are for sale at the local shop in North Mundham. The original has now been hung in the village hall.

A millennium community collage being displayed in St Mary Magdalene and St Denys' church, Midhurst. The collage has been co-ordinated by the parish church under the direction of Julie Carslaw. It features works by all the Midhurst schools and social clubs to show the various activities carried on in the town at the time of the new millennium and will be on display for several months.

Joan Scoular, Sarah Bolton, Lesley Pearce and Mary Hill meet once a month, sometimes with other dedicated needleworkers, in Midhurst with the intention of providing new hassocks for the adjacent village church of Woolbeding. The project, which started eighteen months ago, has now involved at least 20 people making 60 hassocks. It is hoped that all will be finished in early 2000. Gus the cat looks more interested in other matters.

A 'millennium links' exhibition was held in St George's church, Whyke, on the outskirts of Chichester, just before Christmas 1999. The exhibition, involving the four schools in the church parish and directed by the rector Father Paul Seaman, featured a series of nine tableaux around the church showing the different stages in the life of Christ. Money for the event came from fund-raising by members of the parish. The photograph shows pupils of Rumboldswhyke Infants School admiring their own display of the first miracle of Jesus – the wedding at Cana.

Christopher Fry, the poet and dramatist, has lived in East Dean for over 30 years. He is pictured here at a special ceremony to mark the village's new millennium stones, with its youngest inhabitant, six-month-old Zinnia Albery. His associations with Chichester go back to 1939 when he was invited by Bishop Bell to perform his play *The Boy with a Cart* in the grounds of the Bishop's Palace. He was much involved with the foundation of the Festival Theatre and his plays *The Lady's Not for Burning*, *Ring Round the Moon*, and *Venus Observed*, together with his translations of *Peer Gynt* and *Cyrano de Bergerac* have been performed there.

The opening of the new Chichester Cathedral Centre, which provides a designated classroom space for the several thousand school children who visit the cathedral each year. One of the cathedral's official millennium projects, the centre is situated in the ground floor of the treasury building. The opening, described as a very important step by the Dean and Chapter, will enable the cathedral's rich heritage to be passed on to successive generations. The picture shows the Dean of Chichester, the Rt Revd John Treadgold (left) with communar Michael Shallow, retiring education officer Estelle Morgan, education officer Canon Peter Atkinson and architect Richard Meynell.

Helping to turn unused land into a miniature park at Bosham, members of Southbourne Lions present a bench seat as part of the park project organised by Bosham Parish Council to commemorate the millennium. A further bench was provided, as was the planting of 100 daffodil bulbs. The Lions president, Lynn Smith, is shown in suitably relaxed pose!

Valerie Mason shows her collection of Chichester Harbour photographs, mainly taken near Itchenor, to Judi Darley of the Chichester Harbour Conservancy, with the intention of providing material for the Harbour millennium archive project. Having lived most of her life in the Itchenor area, she has many fascinating photographs including some taken during the bitter winter of 1962–63 when the entire harbour was frozen over and boats unable to move for weeks on end.

Just part of the Midhurst Camera Club's millennium project '2,000 Midhurst People'. This scheme has involved the photographing, where possible, of all the residents in Midhurst and the resulting portraits being then displayed on large print panels in Parklands Garage in the centre of North Street for public viewing. Over 2,000 faces are actually shown and copies of individual prints are available for a short period. The negatives will then be handed to the West Sussex County Record Office later in the New Year for posterity.

Rosemary and David Staples studying their personal photographic project of the parish of Singleton. Starting eighteen months ago and helped by neighbours Joy Muir and Liz and John Doff they have taken a photographic record of every permissible house and its occupants in the entire parish and have produced an album that will be presented to the West Sussex County Record Office as a millennium contribution. Not only have nearly all the photographs been taken, but also printed, by David who is an enthusiastic amateur photographer.

Inhabitants from the harbour village of Prinsted gather for a group photograph in the village square on the occasion of the launch of their new book *Prinsted – a Place where Pears Grow*.

In the summer of 1998 a small group from the village decided to form a village history society with the intention of recording the history of Prinsted over the last 100 years in book form as a millennium celebration. Such was the popularity of this project that within a few weeks of the book's publication in late 1999 over 500 copies had been sold and the book had been featured in the local press and television. It is hoped that any profit will later be used for village charities.

The annual Wiley pensioner party in December 1999, just a few days before the start of the new millennium. John Wiley & Sons is one of Chichester's largest employers. The company was founded in New York in 1807 and arrived in Chichester in 1967. As majority shareholders, the Wiley family continues to be involved in the company's day-to-day operations. The family feeling, combined with Chichester's character, its way of life and amenities, has given Wiley a distinct trading advantage over its international competitors. For example, they have been named Publisher of the Year every year since the award's inception in 1996.

At the party, Wiley directors entertained 18 retired employees. Many of these people were among the first staff to join Wiley in 1967. The combined service for the pensioners pictured here is well over 300 years!

The market cross at midnight on 1st January 2000. The new millennium is a few seconds old, and hundreds of people gather around to mark the occasion. Over many centuries the cross has been the focal point for Cicestrians to celebrate the New Year. Around it have also been scenes of commemoration, of national mourning, of the departure of soldiers to various wars and many other events.

Marcus Davies, ringing captain of the bellringers of St Mary Magdalene and St Denys' church, Midhurst, counts down the seconds prior to the celebration bell ringing on New Year's Day at noon. In all, over 35,000 churches throughout the country took part in this special millennium event, some of whose bells were rung for the first time in many years.

There are nine or ten bellringers involved with St Mary Magdalene and St Denys' church, who ring every Sunday and practise fortnightly. Their records go back to 1888. The longest peal of 2 hours 44 minutes was rung as a celebration of their centenary in 1988.

Celebrations at the Hunston fireworks display.

Further celebrations in the Chichester City Club. Chichester City Club is the oldest club in Chichester. When the cathedral spire collapsed in 1861, the Dean of that time, Walter Farquhar Hook, realised that many of the workmen employed on the spire's reconstruction would need some form of club facility within the city. He persuaded the Dean and Chapter to convert 13 North Pallant, then owned by the Chapter, into a working men's club. Established in 1862-3 as the Working Men's Club and Institute, this became the forerunner of the City Club when renamed in 1879. Today the club has over 800 members and is a thriving and popular meeting place.

A group of intrepid bathers at East Wittering beach on New Year's Day. Dressed in a variety of costumes, the swimmers braved the elements to raise money for the HCPT Pilgrimage Trust and other charitable causes.

Grainne Jones with her daughter Frances. Grainne became Chichester's first millennium mother when Frances, weighing 6 lb 9$\frac{1}{2}$ oz was born at 1.31 p.m. on New Year's Day, in St Richard's Hospital. Mrs Jones was presented with a gift voucher and picture frame, by a well-known Chichester jewellers, to celebrate the occasion.

8.00 a.m. 1st January 2000 – the dawn of the new millennium. A grey mist hangs over the stillness of Chichester Harbour at Cutmill Creek. Bosham church can be seen in the distance. Cut Mill itself stood near here, the mill pond being situated just to the north of what is now the A259 road. The mill ceased working in the early 1920s. What further changes will be seen here and elsewhere in the City of Chichester and its surrounding district as the third millennium begins its course?

ACKNOWLEDGEMENTS

We would like to thank the many people who have helped us in the compilation of the book by loaning photographs, allowing photography, being photographed, providing information, and for advising on or contributing captions. We are most grateful to the following for their generous assistance:

Mr H. Adams; Miss L. Adams; Mrs R. Andreae; (Goodwood House); Mr W. Arnell; Mrs V. Asher (Chichester Cathedral Gift Shop); Ballard's Brewery; Mr A. Barnes; Mr J. Bartholomew; Brigadier T. Bevan (Chichester Cathedral Trust); Mrs A. Bone; Miss J. Bowden (Sussex Downs Conservation Board); Mr P. Brears (Petworth House and Cowdray Ruins); Mr J. Buckland and Ms S. Wain (West Dean Gardens); Mrs R. Burkat (St Mary's Hospital); Mr W. Cass (Goodwood Sculpture Park); Revd K.W. Clinch; Mr M. Codd; Mr P. Coleman (New Park Centre); Mr G. Compton (Bignor Roman Villa); Mr J. Cooper (Stansted Park); Mr J. Coppendale (Tangmere Aviation Museum); Revd A. Cunnington; Mr M. Cutten (Ancient Corporation of St Pancras); Miss J. Darley (Chichester Harbour Conservancy); Mr M. Davies; Mr C. Doman; Mr P. Dunnaway; Mr I. Farman (William Mercer); Mr R. Fabricius and Mr S. Buckley (Goodwood Racecourse); Mr R. Fogden; Mr W. Gage (West Sussex County Record Office); Mrs S. Gayford; Mr G. Girling; Great Ballard School; Mr K. Green; Miss A. Griffiths; Mrs L. Grocott; Mr M. Hayes (West Sussex County Council Library Service); Mr M. Hewitt (Strides); Mr L. Holloway; Mr P. Iden; Mr W. Jenman (Sussex Wildlife Trust); Mrs I. Jerome; Mr P. Jerrome (Petworth Cottage Museum); Miss L. Johnson (Pallant House); Mr and Mrs C. Jones (Mechanical Music Museum); Revd E. Knapp-Fisher (St Mary's Hospital); The Bishop of Chichester, the Rt Revd Eric Kemp; Mr I. Kennedy (Noah's Ark Inn); Mr K. Knight; Mr J. Lancaster-Smith; The Landmark Trust; Mr L. Lucas; Mr S. Kitchen (Chichester District Museum); Mr K. Masters (Chichester Cathedral); Mr J. McKerchar (West Wittering Estate); Mr J. Magilton (Alec Down); Mrs G. Miles (Chichester High School for Boys); Mr N. Mitchell (Pitsham Brickworks); Mr R. Morgan; Mrs M. Monnington; Mr P. Morris (Chichester Hospital Radio); Mr D. Morton-Hickson; Mr G. Muffett; Miss C. Orchard (King Edward VII Hospital); Mrs D. Owen (Petworth House); Dr B. Pailthorpe (St Richard's and King Edward VII Hospitals); Miss E. Payce (Chichester District Museum); Mr H. Potter; The Punch House; Mr C. Purchase; Mr N. Purchase; Mrs M. Rapley (Petworth Station); Mr M. Roberts (for Boxgrove Man); Mrs M. Roe; Mr P. Rogerson (Chichester Festival Theatre); Mr D. Rudkin (Fishbourne Roman Palace); Mr I. Russell; Mr D. Sadler (Goodrowes); Mrs S. Saer; Mr S. Sansom; Mr G. Scaife (British School of Ballooning); Mrs J. Scoular; Seaford College; Barrie Seaman Associates and Protodale Ltd (Cawley Almshouses); Father P. Seaman; Mr C. Sharman; Mrs K Shaw; The Ship Hotel; Mrs J. Skelton; Mr C. Skinner; Mr N. Smith; Mr V. Smith (Fittleworth Common); Mr P. Spooner (Rotary Club of Chichester); Mr D. Stenning; Mr J. Stringer (Easebourne); Mrs J. Sutherland; Sir J. Thomas; Mr D. Turner; Mr S. Ward (Edward James Foundation); Mr G. Warren; Westhampnett School; Westbourne House School; Mr and Mrs D. Whitby; Mr R. Widdows (Goodwood Road Racing Company); Mr R. Williamson; Mr R. Windle (Cowdray Estate); Miss L. Younger (Chichester City Council); Mr and Mrs C. Zeuner (Weald and Downland Open Air Museum).

In particular, we would like to thank His Grace the Duke of Richmond and Gordon for writing the Foreword, and whose vision and inspiration it was to produce Chichester: *A Contemporary View*; Mrs S. Fullwood, Principal Curator of Chichester Museum for commissioning the reconstruction paintings by Mike Codd and the advice given by Mr D. Rudkin, Mr M. Taylor (West Sussex County Council Archaeologist) and Mr J. Kenny (Chichester District Council Archaeologist) together with the support of Mr C. Doman, the Bassil Shippam and Alsford Trusts, and Thomas Eggar Church Adams; Mr P. Rogerson and Miss A. Sharp for their assistance over the Chichester Festivities; Mrs J. Price, Mr S. Price and Mr N. Osborne of Phillimore and Co. Ltd for their kind permission to use as a reference and to quote from books by Bernard Price; Dr C. Fry for his kind permission to reproduce his poetry; Mr Karl Dimmock and Mr Keith Newbery, for their help and kind permission to reproduce photographs from the *Chichester Observer*; Mr K. Leslie (West Sussex County Record Office) for all his generous assistance; Joy Whiting and Jane Pailthorpe for their infinite patience, support and much hard work in helping with photographs and typing the manuscript. Finally, our grateful thanks go to Geoff Farrell and Graham Russel of John Wiley & Sons for their support and assistance throughout the project.

Our previous book has been extensively used as a reference source and it is regrettably not possible to mention all those who previously assisted. Our apologies to those that we may on this occasion have unintentionally failed to mention.

REFERENCE SOURCES AND SELECT BIBLIOGRAPHY

There are numerous books, booklets, papers, leaflets and guides about Chichester and the surrounding district. It is an almost impossible task to mention them all, but the following have been most useful and those highlighted have been invaluable as reference sources. It is recommended that anyone interested in seeking more detailed information should refer to them. Mention has also be made, in certain captions, to the various legends and hearsay associated with buildings and places. These, of course, may be founded on fact or fiction, but nevertheless are part of local folklore.

*Arscott, D., *Curiosities of Sussex*, S.B. Publications, 1993

*Armstrong, J.R., *A History of Sussex*, Phillimore, 1995

Bevan, B., *Charles the Second's French Mistress*, Robert Hale, 1972

Bessborough, Earl of, *Enchanted Forest*, Weidenfeld and Nicholson, 1984

*Bishop, J.H., *A Sussex Pot-Pourri*, 1986

Brandon, P., *The Sussex Landscape*, Hodder and Stoughton, 1974

Brandon, P., *The South Downs*, Phillimore, 1998

Bromley-Martin, A., *Around Chichester*, 1991

Bromley-Martin, A., *Chichester Harbour, Past and Present*, Hughenden Publications, 1991

Brown, E., *Chichester in the 1950s*, E.B. Publications, 1996

Brunnarius, M., *Windmills of Sussex*, Phillimore, 1979

Chichester 900, various contributors, Chichester Cathedral, 1975

Chichester District Council guidebooks

The Chichester Harbour Landscape, Countryside Commission

Chichester Hospital Radio Patients Magazine

Chichester Observer Series

Clark, P., *The Chichester and Midhurst Railway*, Turntable Publications, 1979

*Clifton-Taylor, A., *Chichester*, BBC, 1984

*Cobbett, W., *Rural Rides*, Robert Culley, 1909

Coke, D., *Pallant House – Its Architecture, History and Owners*, 1993

Cowdray Park Polo Club *1999 Year Book*

*Dallaway, J., *History of West Sussex, Vols, 1, 2 and 3*, 1815

Done, W.E.P., *Looking Back in Sussex*, Faber and Faber, n.d.

*Down, A., *Roman Chichester*, Phillimore, 1988

*Elliott, A., *Sculpture at Goodwood*, 1998/99

*Evershed-Martin, L., *The Impossible Theatre*, Phillimore, 1971

*Fowler, D., *A Conservation Plan for Cowdray Ruins*, produced by Broadway Malyan

Frost, R., *Chichester at the Millennium*, Summersdale, 1999

*Gage, W., Harris, M., Sullivan, A., *Going off the Rails*, West Sussex County Council, 1997

Garland, P., *Angels in the Sussex Air*, Sinclair-Stevenson, 1995

Gittings, R., *John Keats*, Penguin Books, 1968

Glover, J., *Sussex Place Names*, Countryside Books, 1997

Godfrey, J., Leslie, K., Zeuner, D., *Very Special County: West Sussex County Council, The First 100 Years*, West Sussex County Council, 1988

Goodwood Papers, West Sussex County Record Office

*Green, K., *Chichester Remembered*, Ensign Publications, 1989

Green, K., *The Street Names of Chichester*, Verdant Press, 1996

Guy, J., *Castles in Sussex*, Phillimore, 1984

*Guides and leaflets to: *Bepton, Chithurst, Church Norton, Didling, Eartham, Selham and Upwaltham churches, Boxgrove and Shulbrede Priories, Archaeology in West Sussex, Centurion Way Railway Path, Birdham Pool, Chichester canal, Chichester Cathedral, Donaldson's Flowers Ltd, East Head Sand Dunes, Fishbourne Roman Palace, Goodwood House, Hazlewood VHB, Petworth Cottage Museum, Petworth House Roussillon Barracks, St Mary's Hospital, Tangmere Aviation Museum, Weald and Downland Open Air Museum, Wey and Arun canal.*

Harmer, R., *Chichester in Old Photographs*, Alan Sutton, 1990

Heneghan, F.D., *The Chichester Canal*, Chichester Papers, 1958

Hepworth, M., *A Sussex Village, Story of Lurgashall over 2000 Years*, 1991

Hill, A., *The Family Fortune*, SCAN Books, 1978

*Hobbs, M., *Chichester Cathedral – An Historical Survey*, Phillimore, 1994

*Howard-Bailey, C., *St Richard's Hospital, an Oral History*, Phillimore, 1998

*Hudson, W.H., *Nature in Downland*, J M Dent, 1923

*Hunn, D., *Goodwood*, Davis-Poynter, 1975

*Jerrome, P, *The Men with Laughter in their Hearts*, Window Press, 1986

*Johnson-Davies, F., *Midhurst – A Brief History*, Midhurst Society, 1996

*Keating, L., *The Book of Chichester*, Barracuda Books, 1979

*Large, S E, *King Edward VII Hospital, Midhurst 1901–1986*, Phillimore, 1986

Lee, C., *From the Sea End*, Partridge Press, 1989

*Leslie, K., Short, B., *An Historical Atlas of Sussex*, Phillimore, 1999

*Lucas, E.V., *Highways and Byways in Sussex*, Macmillan, 1904

Marshall, J., *Sussex Cricket, A History*, Heinemann, 1959

*McCann, A., *A Short History of the City of Chichester and its Cathedral*, WSRO, 1985

*McCann, A. and McCann T.J., *A Short History of Greyfriars and Priory Park*, Chichester District Museum, 1996

*McCann T.J., *Restricted Grandeur*, Chichester, 1586–1948, WSRO, 1974

*Magilton, J., *The Archaeology of Chichester and District 1996 and 1997, Papers on Chichester, the Burghal Hidage and the diversion of the River Lavant and the Origin and Growth of Midhurst*

*Meade-Fetherstonhaugh, M., and Warner, O., *Uppark and its People*, George Allen and Unwin, 1964

Mee, A., *Sussex*, Hodder and Stoughton, 1937

Mee, F., *A History of Selsey*, Phillimore, 1988

Midhurst Town Council Official Guide and Town Map 1999–2000

*Morgan, R., *Chichester – A Documentary History*, Phillimore, 1992

Morris, J., *The History of the Selsey Lifeboats*, RNLI, 1986

*Nairn, I., and Pevsner, N., *The Buildings of England: Sussex*, Penguin Books, 1975

*Newbery, K., *The River Lavant*, Phillimore, 1987

Ogley, R., Currie, I., Davison, M., *The Sussex Weather Book*, Froglets Publications, 1991

Ollernshaw, P., *The History of Prebendal School*, Phillimore, 1984

Owen, D., *Petworth, The Servants' Quarters*, National Trust, 1997

Palmer, R., *Heyshott – 2000 BC- 2000 AD*, Heyshott History Society, 1999

Pailthorpe, R., Serraillier, I., *Goodwood Country in Old Photographs*, Alan Sutton, 1987

*Pailthorpe, R., McGowan, I., *Chichester: A Contemporary View*, John Wiley & Sons, 1994

Petworth Society Magazines, Vols 30, 31, 32

Pitts, M., Roberts, M., *Fairweather Eden*, Century, 1997

*Price, B., *Sussex, People, Places and Things*, Phillimore, 1975

*Price, B., *Bygone Chichester*, Phillimore, 1975

*Price, B., *The Valiant Years*, Phillimore, 1978

*Price, B., *Changing Chichester*, Phillimore, 1982

Rees, S., *The Charlton Hunt*, Phillimore, 1998

Reese, M.M., *Goodwood's Oak*, Threshold, 1987

*Reger, J., *Chichester Harbour – A History*, Phillimore, 1986

*Rowell, C., Robinson, J.M., *Uppark Restored*, National Trust, 1996

Sarginson, P. (Ed.), *The Edward James Foundation*, 1992

Scott, H., *Secret Sussex*, Batchworth Press, 1949

Serraillier, I., *All Change at Singleton*, Phillimore, 1979

Smith, W.J., *Sussex Smugglers*, Brighton

The Smith Brothers of Chichester, Friends of Pallant House, 1986

Steer, F.W., *The Dolphin and Anchor Hotel*, Chichester Papers, No. 23, 1960

*Steer, F.W., *The Memoirs of James Spershott*, Chichester Papers, No. 30, 1962

Steer, F.W., *The Grange, Tower Street*, Chichester Papers, No. 39, 1963

Sussex Archaeological Collections, Vols 117, 119, *Papers on the Mound at Church Norton* by F. Aldsworth

*Swinfen, W., Arscott, D., *Hidden Sussex*, BBC Radio Sussex, 1984

Thomas, J., *The Rhythm of the Tide*, SMH Books, 1999

Uden, G., *A History of Strides*

The Victoria County History of Sussex, Vols 3 and 4, Dawsons of Pall Mall and Oxford University Press, 1953 and 1973

Vine, P.A.L., *London's Lost Route to the Sea*, David and Charles, 1965

Vigar, J.E., *The Lost Villages of Sussex*, Dovecot Press, 1994

Wales, A., *Landscapes of West Sussex*, Ensign Publications, 1994

Wales, A., *West Sussex Village Book*, Countryside Books, 1984

Westhampnett, from the Ice Age to the Romans, Trust for Wessex Archaeology Ltd, 1992

Williamson, R., *The Great Yew Forest*, Macmillan, 1978

*Willis, T.G., *Records of Chichester*, 1928

Wilson, A.E., *Archaeology of the City Walls*, Chichester Papers, No. 6, 1957

Displays at the Chichester District Museum and their millennium exhibition Chichester – A Century of Change, and at the West Sussex County Record Office's exhibition The Boer War – A Centenary Exhibition.